Replacement Theology

Critical Issues Concerning the History, Doctrine, and Dangers of Replacement Theology

Replacement Theology

Critical Issues Concerning the History, Doctrine,
and Dangers of Replacement Theology

DAVID DUNLAP

REPLACEMENT THEOLOGY: CRITICAL ISSUES CONCERNING
THE HISTORY, PRINCIPLES, AND DANGERS OF REPLACEMENT
THEOLOGY
By: David Dunlap
Copyright © 2012
David Dunlap

Bible & Life Ministries, Inc.
David Dunlap
3116 Gulfwind Drive
Land O' Lakes, FL 34639
(813) 996-1053
daviddunlap@earthlink.net

Published by
GOSPEL FOLIO PRESS
304 Killaly St. W.
Port Colborne, ON L3K 6A6
CANADA

ISBN: 9781926765877

Cover design by Danielle Elzinga

All Scripture quotations from the
King James Version unless otherwise noted.

Printed in USA

A terrific manuscript. Wonderfully written. Thank you for the opportunity to read it and offer suggestions. Again, a great job. I pray that the Lord will use your book to His honor and glory. Blessings.

Bruce Scott, Friends of Israel
New Hope, Minnesota

This book clearly identifies the distinction between the church and Israel and their promises. The interesting historical facts and the chapter and verse documentation for the truths set forth will fill an important need.

Jim Thompson, New England Bible Sales
Augusta, Maine

I thoroughly enjoyed your book and your detailed historical background of events. It boggled my mind and brought me into the wonder of God's promises, which have never failed!

Pei Ling Chin
Kajang, Malaysia

David Dunlap had rendered a great service to the church by warning them about a segment of the "Christian" community who is intent on obliterating the future of Israel. The transgression in the whole discussion boils down to throwing out the Word of God as the Word of God. To remove from the Scriptures the promises to Israel is to convolute the hermeneutics of prophesy, which if done to the gospel would render our message meaningless. What is at stake in these arguments is *"Thus says the Lord…"*

Fred Kosin
Author of *Blessings All Mine With 10,000 Besides*

In this timely new work, David Dunlap appeals to sound biblical doctrine and discernment to defend against the aggressive inroads of the unbiblical doctrines of Supersessionism or Replacement Theology into the church. As he states, "age does not improve doctrinal quality." From the early centuries of the church until today, Replacement Theology has denied a future for ethnic, national Israel, which is a jab in the "apple of God's eye," His covenant people Israel. This is dangerous territory to tread. May God use this book to encourage believers in their discernment and understanding of God's unchangeable promises He made to Israel for a glorious reign of Messiah in a restored land, a regenerated ethnic Israel, fulfilling the Abrahamic, Land, Davidic, and New Covenant to Israel, His Glory!

Jon Yeager
Ridge Manor, Florida

Replacement Theology as a growing opinion among many Christians is clearly the result of thinking that is rooted in a misinterpretation of Scripture and a host of inaccurate assumptions. Such a misguided approach to understanding the Bible has not only generated much confusion regarding God's plan for the nation of Israel, but since its inception it has fueled the horrific evil of anti-Semitism. In this timely volume, David Dunlap explores the origins, development, and ramifications of this spiritually deviant doctrine. It is a must reading and much needed resource for the Lord's people.

Michael Gentile, Carrollwood Bible Chapel
Tampa, Florida

Replacement Theology by David Dunlap is a comprehensive introductory survey of the pertinent issues arising from God's programme in the distinction between Israel as a nation and the New Testament church. An informative book that challenges us to check the theological framework of our choice in the hermeneutical method, its processes and its ministry implications for the local church in its witness and testimony.

Anthony Too, Elder, Jalan Imbi Chapel
Kuala Lampur, Malaysia

Table of Contents

Part I

Part II: Short Papers

Preface

The relationship between Israel and the church continues to be a controversial topic. Anyone who has an interest in the doctrines relating to Israel, the church, and Scriptures relating to the endtimes prophecy is probably aware of this fact. At the heart of this controversy is the question, does God have a future plan for the nation of Israel? Or has God set aside Israel is such a way that now the church fulfills all the promises God has made to Israel. The name to which Bible students have given to this subject is "Replacement Theology" or as Bible scholars call it; "Supersessionism." This topic is not an academic thesis for proponents and opponents to debate in the ivory towers of higher learning. No, this is a topic that will affect the way we view and understand many of the important doctrines of Christianity. Some of these doctrines include: End-times prophecy, the nature and mission of the church, and the art and science of Bible interpretation, and the love of God. This book is an effort to explain some of the important issues that are at stake and its dangers and consequences. My goal in this book is not to offend those who may have other views on the subject. I do not desire to engender more strife but to provide a book that will be a help and encouragement to interested Christians.

I would like to say at the outset that while there are many aspects to consider when it comes to the subject of Israel and the church, yet I believe the Bible teaches that God has not set Israel aside but has a wonderful plan for her future. In a future day God will save, restore, and re-gather Israel according to His Word and for His glory. Some of the material in this book has been taken, reworked, and revised from two of my earlier works, *Limiting Omnipotence* and *The Glory of the Ages*.

I would like to express my thanks to a number of friends who have profitably read, commented upon, and critiqued earlier versions of this work. Fred Kosin for his review and his writing of the foreword to this book. Jim Thompson, of New England Bible Sales for his thoughtful review of this book. Bruce Scott, of Friends of Israel Gospel Ministry, in Minneapolis, MN, has reviewed this work and has made many helpful suggestions. I would like to thank my beloved wife, Faith, for her sacrificial labors in proofreading the initial drafts of this book.

David Dunlap
Land O' Lakes, Florida
2012

Foreword

A Baptist pastor phoned me recently and asked, "Do you think God is through with Israel?" My reply was, "Do you want God to be as faithful to His promises to you as some folks think He will be to Israel?" "Thanks", he said. "That's all I need to know" and he hung up the phone." David Dunlap's work on "Replacement Theology" is both timely and necessary. He examines this aberration of biblical doctrine in a scholarly way through consistent exegesis, thorough examination of church history and constraining arguments. *This volume serves as a strong corrective, for the damage inflicted on the community of faith, by the virulence of "Replacement Theology." Anyone who will give careful attention to Dunlap's presentation against this heresy will be helped to understand the seriousness of the conflict.* Adhering to the tenets of "Replacement Theology" he says calls into question the veracity of the Scriptures, the faithfulness of the God of Israel, the literal grammatical interpretation of prophecy and the spiritual blessings for the Church of God.

The Holy Spirit through the pen of the Apostle Paul gives the divine distinction of the peoples of the world as "...*the Jews, or to the Greeks* (Gentiles) *or to the church of God.*" (I Cor. 10:32) All of mankind falls within this threefold division. Of course this distinction was not possible until the Church was born on the day of Pentecost. Before that historic event humanity was designated as only the Jew and the Gentile. From the beginning of man's dwelling on earth until God chose Abraham, mankind was composed of the nations of the world.

The Bible is the history and prophesies of these three groups of people. The position of importance varies as is evidenced by the amount of space the scriptures devote to each segment of the population. Eleven chapters from Genesis 1-11 envelope 2000 years of history of the nations of the world. The rest of the

Old Testament is devoted to the nation of Israel, its development and divisions, patriarchs and promises, laws and rebellions, scattering and regathering. It is clear from reading this portion of Scripture that God put His imprimatur on the children of Israel as His People and He as their God.

Without reading the New Testament no one would conclude that the God of Israel would be unfaithful in fulfilling His covenants, His promises and His purposes to His people Israel. One might read the Gospels for the first time with great anticipation to see how the "Lord God of Israel" would work out His plan for blessing His people. We might ask "How and when the Messiah of Israel would come and what He would do for His nation." But with the introduction of the Church in the New Testament it seems that man's corrupt mind cannot retain the fulfillment of the blessings to Israel and at the same time see the same person blessing the spiritual organism called "the church of Jesus Christ."

The distinction between "the Church of God" and "the Israel of God" is a divinely sanctioned designation that unfolds to the mind that is spiritually energized by the Holy Spirit. To say that God will be faithful to the nations of the world who reject Christ because they "will be turned into hell" and that all the promises to the church such as "so shall we ever be with the Lord" will be literally fulfilled and affirm that the same God will not fulfill the hundreds of promises to Israel is to reject the words of God's Word and convolute the simple meaning of the texts of the Scriptures.

David Dunlap has presented this excellent work defending the distinction between the promises of God to Israel and those to His church. His assessment of the popularly described "Replacement Theology" is adequately defended from history, accurately described from writings, ably defined by various authors and affirmably shattered from the Scriptures. To continue to hold to "Replacement Theology" after reading this expose is to reject sound reasoning, seasoned scholarship, sensible interpretation of the Bible and the enlightenment of the Holy Spirit and fall into a liberal view of God and His Word.

Foreword

May this ground breaking work be used of God to enrich the Israel of God, strengthen the hope of the church of God, elevate our view of the Bible and embolden Christians to realize that as His church we worship the "God of Israel" and therefore cannot be anti-Semitic or reject the future of God's people Israel on earth reflected in the Scriptures. Jesus Christ is "King of kings" to Israel and "Lord of lords" to the church. To Him be Glory forever and ever!

Fredrick Kosin
Author and Bible teacher
Darlington, South Carolina
2012

What is Replacement Theology?

For the past 150 years, the evangelical church has given great emphasis to God's promises to the nation of Israel. Christians were those who rejoiced the loudest when Israel became a nation on May 14, 1948. Evangelical Christians understood that God would be faithful to these irrevocable promises to Israel. As the ever-faithful God, He has bound Himself to His Word! He will not forsake His people. The apostle Paul reminds us, *"I say then, hath God cast away His people? God forbid"* (Rom. 11:1). However, in recent years, more and more Christian leaders are beginning to turn their backs on Israel. Popular Christian radio preacher Hank Hanegraaf argues in his 2006 book *Apocalypse Code* that Israel has no future in the plan of God. Reformed writer Keith Mathison, in his 2010 book *Post-Millennialism: Eschatology of Hope,* denies that God will fulfill His promises to Israel. In a recent sermon on Romans chapter eleven, popular Calvinistic Bible teacher John Piper stated:

> The promises made to Abraham, including the promise of the Land, will be inherited as an everlasting gift only by true, spiritual Israel, not disobedient, unbelieving Israel. In other words, the promises cannot be demanded by anyone just because he is Jewish... Being born Jewish does not make one an heir of the promise – neither the promise of the Land nor any other promise.[1]

Popular Christian leaders, such as R. C. Sproul, Gary DeMar, John Piper, and others, argue that because Israel has been unfaithful to God, these Old Testament promises are now given to Christians. This doctrine is called Replacement Theology or

"Supersessionism" by Bible scholars and academics. Replacement Theology is the view that the Church has permanently replaced or superseded Israel as the people of God. The Church will inherit all these Old Testament promises. In recent years, Replacement Theology has gained more and more popularity among evangelical Christians. Down through history, Replacement Theology has been the unfortunate fuel that has energized violent anti-Semitism, Eastern European pogroms, the Holocaust, and contemporary disdain for the modern state of Israel.

Definition and Description

Replacement Theology teaches that God has rescinded all his promises to Israel, and those promises have been given to the Church. Renald Showers explains:

> Replacement Theology is a theological view of the world that claims God is forever finished with Israel as a nation. Therefore, God's promises in the Abrahamic Covenant to give the physical descendants of Abraham, Isaac, and Jacob the land of Canaan as an eternal inheritance are no longer in effect with national Israel.[2]

According to this view, God is finished with Israel and is now working with the Church of God. Of course, all Christians believe that the Church is the primary agent that God is using in the present church age, but we must never forget that God has a future plan in which He will restore national Israel to a place of blessing and usefulness in the world.

Replacement leaders teach that the Church of Jesus Christ replaces racial, national Israel and becomes God's sole focus for the rest of biblical time. Israel has no future in the plan of God. All the blessings of Israel in the Old and New Testaments have become the blessings of the Church.

Dr. Walter Kaiser, a professor at Gordon-Conwell Theological Seminary, explains the nature of Replacement Theology. He writes:

Replacement Theology...declared that the Church, Abraham's spiritual seed, had replaced national Israel in that it had transcended and fulfilled the terms of the covenant given to Israel, which covenant Israel had lost because of disobedience.[3]

Another writer Ronald E. Diprose, explains:

The Church completely and permanently replaced ethnic Israel in the working out of God's plan and as recipient of Old Testament promises addressed to Israel. [4]

Replacement theologians teach that Israel's best days are in her past and she has no future in the plan of God. The Church inherits all the blessings, while Israel is meant to endure only curses.

The Rise of Replacement Theology

The New Testament Church began in the decade between A.D. 30 and 40 of the first century. It was first centered in Jerusalem and, initially, was predominantly Jewish. Many of these early Jewish believers had little desire to turn their backs on Judaism. They saw Christianity as a fulfillment, not the enemy, of the faith of Abraham, Isaac, and Jacob. They expected that all Jews would embrace Jesus of Nazareth as the true Messiah as they had. Sadly, the majority of the Jews would reject Christ and, in time, would take up arms to severely persecute the early Christians. This persecution forced these Christians to scatter to nearby cities and villages. As a result, many Samaritans and Gentiles were reached with the gospel. Within a short period of time, the Church turned from being overwhelmingly Jewish to being predominantly Gentile. These Gentile believers did not view the Old Testament promises to Israel with the same passion as the early Jewish believers. These Gentile Christians began to teach that because the Jewish people, by and large, had rejected God, God had rejected them, and the Church now had become the chosen people. They claimed that God had permanently ended His unique relationship with Israel and replaced it with the Church.

By the second century, Replacement Theology had become entrenched in the minds of many Christian leaders. Although the church leaders at this time were predominantly pre-millennial in their understanding of future things, they embraced the idea of Replacement Theology. Early Christian apologist Justin Martyr (A.D. 100-165) was one of the first to write circa A.D. 160 that the Christian Church was the true spiritual Israel. In a work called *Dialogue of Justin Martyr With Trypho a Jew*, he explained that Christians are the true Israelite race and that the "seed of Jacob," when properly understood referred to Christians and not to Jews. Justin's views laid the groundwork for the growing belief that the Church had replaced Israel. By the end of the third century, this teaching had become entrenched in most of the churches in Europe and the Middle East.

Today, the majority of non-evangelical churches have embraced Replacement Theology. Roman Catholic churches since the time of Augustine have rigidly held to this view, along with Lutheran, Presbyterian, Anglican, Methodist, and most Reformed and Calvinistic denominations. Nevertheless, for the last 150 years, Dispensational and Evangelical Bible churches have vigorously resisted the inroads of Replacement Theology. However, in recent years, this wall of separation between Replacement Theology and the Dispensational-Evangelical church has been breached. Today, popular Evangelical leaders and Bible teachers have embraced and are promoting Replacement Theology. Christian leaders, such as R. C. Sproul, and Christian broadcaster Hank Hanegraaf, along with a host of other influential leaders, are happily teaching this doctrine. The Emerging Church movement is at the forefront in the advance of Replacement Theology.

The Impact Of Replacement Theology

Replacement Theology has had a devastating effect on the Jewish people, as well as on many important biblical doctrines.

From its earliest days to the present time, Replacement Theology has been a catalyst for violence and anti-Semitic attitudes in the Church. Replacement Christians, since the third century, have been active in persecuting the Jewish people throughout the world. This persecution first began under anti-Semitic Roman Catholic leaders. Later, Lutherans led by the reformer Martin Luther were involved in stirring up horrific acts of anti-Jewish violence. Some of the worst persecution of the Jewish people came at this time.

In this book we will show this view was also the impetus for unsound doctrine in the Church. Replacement Theology has led to the formation of state churches, the allegorizing of Scripture, the organization of religious armies, the sacrifice of the Mass (Transubstantiation), and the separation of the church into unbiblical clergy and laity classes. This led former Professor of Systematic Theology at Wheaton College, Henry Thiessen, to write:

> While there is a connection between the saved of all ages, Christianity is new wine poured into new wineskins. What mischief has been done by the Roman Catholic Church through its attempt to continue the Levitical system of the Old Testament! Tertullian was the first to call ministers, priests; and Cyprian the first to introduce the idea that the mass was a sacrifice. Thus great sanctuaries and an elaborate ritual were introduced into the church to replace the simple meeting places of earlier times, and the unadorned preaching of the gospel in primitive Christianity.[5]

Conclusion

Although Replacement Theology has had its champions in the Church since the second century, in this case, age does not improve doctrinal quality. Replacement Theology has corrupted and degraded both the Church's doctrine and practice.

Replacement Theology has resulted in some of the darkest periods of persecution and anti-Semitism. Today, in many ways, Preterism, Covenant theology, Amillennialism, and Calvinism continue this unfortunate tradition of prejudice and unsound Bible doctrine. In this short volume, we will seek to explain the dangers of Replacement Theology while exhorting Christians to be faithful to Bible doctrine and sensitive to the Jewish people.

Endnotes

1. www.desiringgod.org/resource-library/sermons/israel-palestine-and-the-middle-east (March 7, 2004)

2. Renald Showers, *The Coming Apocalypse*, (Bellmawr, NJ: Friends of Israel, 2010), p. 7-8

3. Quoted in Michael Vlach, *Has the Church Replaced Israel?*, (Nashville, TN: B & H Academic, 2010), p. 11

4. Ronald E. Diprose, *Israel and the Church: The Origin and Effects of Replacement Theology*, (Waynesboro, GA: Authentic Media, 2004), p. 2

5. Henry C. Thiessen, *Lectures in Systematic Theology*, (Grand Rapids, MI: Eerdmans, 1976), p. 405

Key Events in the History of Replacement Theology

Edward Gibbon, the famous chronicler of the Roman Empire, has said, "History is little more than the register of the crimes, follies, and misfortunes of mankind." A poet once said, "He who does not learn from history is doomed to repeat it." When Oliver Cromwell was planning the education of his son Richard, he said, "I would have him learn a little history." The Bible says, *"Now these things happened to them as an example and were written for our instruction"* (1 Cor. 10:11). From the beginning of time, history has been mankind's greatest teacher. Of all the nations of the world, the history of the Jewish people has been one of the best chronicled, the most studied, and yet, by many, the least appreciated. From the second century, the history of the Jewish people and the history of Replacement Theology can be described as two train rails laid side by side. Since the time Replacement ideas became a settled teaching, its leaders have been a barb in the side of the descendants of Abraham, Isaac, and Jacob. In this chapter we will explore the history of the Jewish people and key events in the history of Replacement Theology.

Gentile Composition of the Church

Replacement Theology began to gain a foothold in the early Church when the church slowly changed in composition from a majority of Jewish believers to a predominance of Gentile converts. In it's early years, the New Testament Church was composed almost exclusively of Jewish believers. One would not be far off the mark to say that the first generation of the church was "Jewish-Christian." The apostles were all Jewish, the Lord Jesus Christ was Jewish, and the earliest followers of Christ were

Jewish, so it is no surprise that the church was overwhelmingly Jewish. These Jewish believers had a great appreciation for the Old Testament promises to national Israel. However, after the apostles died, the next generation of leaders were mostly Gentile, and the great centers of Christian growth were in the Gentile cites of Rome, Alexandria, and Antioch. The Church, which began as a predominantly Jewish movement, slowly became largely non-Jewish by the second century. The new Gentile church leaders had less and less appreciation for God's unique plan for the Jewish nation. By the second century, these leaders began to teach that God was finished with the nation of Israel, and the Church would inherit all the Old Testament promises made to Israel.

Two Jewish revolts against Rome in the first and second centuries accelerated the Gentile growth of the Church. In A.D. 66-73 and A.D. 132-135, the Jewish leadership revolted against their Roman oppressors. In A.D. 70, the revolt was led by Shimon bar Giora and in A.D. 132 by Shimon Bar Kokhba, "son of a star", a false messiah. The Roman army eventually crushed both of these revolts. Afterward, many Jews sought refuge outside Jerusalem, thereby weakening the Jewish influence on the church. According to church historian Eusebius (A.D. 263-339), prior to the revolt in A.D. 132-135, there were 15 Jewish-Christians who occupied official leadership roles in the church in Jerusalem. In a relatively short time after the revolt, there were no Jewish leaders, and the Gentile-Christian Marcus took on the leading role in the church.

The Destruction of Jerusalem

In the Jewish revolt against Rome in A.D. 66-73, the fighting centered in Jerusalem and Judea and in other areas of heavy Jewish population. The Roman general Vespasian had begun the Roman conquest in northern Israel. After three years of war, he was recalled to Rome, and his son general Titus took over. General Titus was a more vicious and ruthless military leader than his father before him. In A.D. 70, after several months of intense fighting, the city of Jerusalem was taken and the temple destroyed. Tens of thousands of Jews were killed with the sword, died of starvation, or were enslaved. Today in Rome, the famous "Arch of Titus" depicts the golden lampstand, which was taken from the temple, being carried away to Rome.

In the second major Jewish revolt, from A.D. 132-135, hundreds of Jewish villages joined in the bitter fight. The Romans called Julius Serverus from Britain to come and crush the rebellion. More than half a million Jews perished in this revolt and nearly all of Judea lay in ruins. The Romans destroyed Jerusalem completely; every wall was leveled and the city plowed under. The Romans built a new city, which was called "Aelia Capitolina" in honor of the Roman emperor Aelious Hadrianus (A.D. 76-138). A temple dedicated to Jupiter was built on the site of the former Jewish temple. All Jews were forbidden to enter Aelia upon pain of death, and the new city was repopulated with Greek-speaking Gentiles. The land of Israel, for the first time, was named "Palestina" in an attempt to further rid Israel of all Jewish character.

Rome's crushing defeat of two national revolts within sixty years had far-reaching consequences for the Jewish people. These defeats spelled death for Israel's temple worship, national pride, and her spiritual life.

In a short period of time, Christians began to view the destruction of Jerusalem in A.D. 70 and A.D. 135 as God's judgment against Israel. Christian apologist Justin Martyr argued in his *Dialogue with Typho* circa A.D. 160 that these destructions of Jerusalem were God's judgment on the Christ-rejecting Jews. He stated that Jews "justly suffer" and that the Jewish cities were rightly "burned with fire."[1]

Early Church leader Origen (A.D. 185-254) was even more severe in his criticism of the Jewish people. He wrote concerning the destructions of Jerusalem:

> For what nation is an exile from their own metropolis, and from the place sacred to the worship of their fathers, save the Jews alone? And these calamities they have suffered because they were a most wicked

nation, which, although guilty of many other sins, yet punished so severely for none, as for those that were committed against our Jesus.[2]

The early Church fathers unanimously concluded that the destruction of Jerusalem and the dispersion of the Jewish people into the surrounding nations demonstrated that God had clearly rejected the Jews, and that Christians now had become the "New Israel."

The Origin of Allegorical Interpretation

In the latter part of the first century, Replacement leaders struggled with the strong Jewish character of the Old Testament Scriptures. Their anti-Jewish stance forced them to view the Old Testament with suspicion, for they taught that the Church had replaced Israel. They realized that their position created a difficult theological dilemma. If they were to promote the Old Testament, it would reinforce and remind readers that Israel was unique and still had a special place in the divine plan of God. If they were to reject the Old Testament Scriptures, they would be rejecting God's revelation to Abraham and Moses, the wisdom books, the poetic books, and the prophets. They struggled to find a remedy to this dilemma.

Marcion (A.D. 85-160), an early Replacement leader, offered a solution. He violently opposed anything Jewish and argued that the Old Testament should be removed from the canon of Scripture. Although many were sympathetic to this viewpoint, the church could not cut itself off from the Jewish Scriptures. If there were no Old Testament Scriptures, what then did the Church replace? If there were no promises of God, what promises would they inherit in place of Israel? Furthermore, the Old Testament Scriptures were filled with hundreds of Messianic prophecies that were fulfilled by Jesus Christ in the New Testament. The Church rightly rejected Marcion's extreme suggestion. In its place, it found an alternative solution—allegory.

Clement (A.D. 150-210) of Alexandria, Egypt devoted himself to the allegorical interpretation of Scripture. He was considered to be the "father" of allegorical interpretation. Later his disciple, Origen (A.D. 184-254) carried this principle a step when he suggested numerous doctrines build upon allegorical interpretation. In allegory, the Old Testament could be transformed from a Jewish book into a "Christian" book. Through their efforts to spiritualize and allegorize the text, the early Church fathers were able to "find" abundant Christian teaching in the Jewish Scriptures. The Lord Jesus Christ and New Testament teachings were read *into* rather than *out of* the biblical text in the most obscure places. As a result, Irenaeus, Origen, Tertullian, Augustine, and others developed a system of allegorical interpretation that had the disastrous effect of distorting biblical passages from their plain meaning. During the Reformation, Martin Luther called Origen's allegorical interpretation a "nose of wax" that could bend the Scriptures any way one desired.

Allegory enabled Replacement leaders of the early Church to replace Old Testament Jewish ritual with the New Testament Church counterpart. For example, the sacrifices of the Old Testament became the bread and wine of the Lord's Supper, and the twelve bells on the robe of the high priest now signified the twelve disciples. The scarlet cord of Rahab was interpreted as salvation through the blood of Christ. Noah symbolized Christ and the ark, the Church. The Old Testament was robbed of its rich and elegant meaning.

The history of biblical interpretation proves that, at best, allegorical interpretation is both suspect and risky. The plain and obvious meaning of the text is surrendered to the opinion and bias of the interpreter. The intended meaning of Abraham, Moses, Jesus, or Paul will be lost when we seek a mystical, figurative, or hidden meaning in Scripture.

Historians have noted that one sad result of an allegorical method of interpretation is a greater feeling of anti-Semitism among Christians. Respected Christian thinker and former professor at Trinity Evangelical Divinity School, Dr. Harold O. J. Brown, has observed that Christians have tended to be more hostile to Jewish people as they inclined toward a more

25

allegorical method of Bible interpretation. He further argued that since the Church took on an Amillennial viewpoint from the time of Augustine, there has been an increasing disdain for the Jewish people.[3]

Dangers of Allegorical Interpretation

There is another thorny issue regarding allegory that must be pointed out. Among the most troubling consequences of allegorized interpretation is the weakening of the authority of Scripture. Some Bible scholars have pointed out the link between a spiritualized-allegorical method of interpretation and the denial of both biblical inerrancy and the plenary-verbal inspiration of Scripture. How does this come about? The underlying reason is that allegorical interpretation reinforces the belief that Scripture does not mean what it plainly says. If the Old Testament promises to Israel simply do not mean what they clearly state; if God is not faithful to the words of His covenant to Israel; if He is not true to His word to Abraham, Isaac, and Jacob, can we also trust what the New Testament teaches? What about the miraculous accounts in the Old and New Testaments—should they be allegorically interpreted? By considering these and other questions, one can see the serious theological consequences that can result. One such consequence is the downward slide into modernism and theological liberalism. There are many Amillennial and Reformed believers that strongly believe in the authority of Holy Scripture. However, we would be remiss if we did not point out that church denominations that are Amillennial or Reformed are among the most liberal and modernistic. On the other hand, church denominations that are more literal in their interpretation of Scripture are usually faithful to the fundamentals of the faith. At the heart of modernism is the conviction that the Bible is merely a collection of fables, moral stories, and ethical teachings. In time, Amillennial non-literal hermeneutics will lead to modernism, or will at least weaken convictions concerning plenary-verbal inspiration and the inerrancy of the Scriptures. Dr. Charles Ryrie observes:

Allegorical interpretation fosters modernism. As has often been pointed out, it is almost impossible to find a pre-millennial liberal or modernist. Among (Plymouth) Brethren, who are supposed to be the founders of modern literalism, liberalism is practically unknown. On the other hand, the great body of modernistic Protestantism is avowed amillennial. Thus, the allegorical method of amillennialism is a step toward modernism. [4]

Martin Luther and the Reformation

Martin Luther's views concerning Jews and Judaism have been the subject of much debate. Many believe that Luther, at the beginning of the Reformation, spoke thoughtfully and kindly about the Jews. Luther prayed for the Jews, and in his sermons he exhorted Christians to be kind and friendly towards them. He once said, "We ought, therefore, not to treat Jews unkindly, for there are many future Christians among them." In 1523, he wrote a book called *That Jesus Was Born a Jew*, in which he suggested that many Jews would embrace the Lord Jesus Christ and convert to Christianity. He wrote, "Many of them will become genuine Christians and turn again to the faith of their fathers, the prophets, and the patriarchs." He had hoped that the conversion of the Jews might also be a turning point in the Reformation in Europe.

However, Luther's attitude toward the Jews changed dramatically near the end of his ministry. From 1530 to the end of his life, the tone in his writings toward the Jews became harsher and more negative. He became less optimistic about the conversion of the Jewish people to Christianity. Luther's strongest statements against the Jewish people occurred in 1543, the last year of his life. He wrote a tract entitled *Concerning the Jews and Their Lies*. In this tract, he called the Jews "a miserable and accused people." In his latter writings, he also took a strong Replacement view concerning the Jews. He believed that God had rejected them as a nation, and the Church was now the chosen people of God. He viewed the destruction of Jerusalem and the Temple in A.D. 70 as evidence of God's permanent rejection of Israel. He wrote:

> Listen, Jew, are you aware that Jerusalem and your sovereignty, together with your temple and priesthood, have been destroyed 1,460 years ago?... This work of wrath is proof that the Jews, surely rejected by God, are no longer His people and neither is He any longer their God.[5]

Luther concluded that the church and the Christian are now the true people of God. The destruction of the city of Jerusalem and the Temple were proof that God had entirely rejected the Jewish people as the people of God. The Jewish people were now without hope and God in the world.

Israel, Anti-Semitism, and "Christian Reconstructionism"

In the early 1970s, a revival of Replacement Theology ideas began to influence many evangelical Christians. This movement was called "Christian Reconstructionism" or "Dominion Theology." The movement was founded in the United States and popularized by Rousas John Rushdoony in his work *The Institutes of Biblical Law* (1973). As a controversial and unorthodox figure, Rushdoony drew much criticism for his views. Other significant Reconstructionist leaders included Gary North (Rushdoony's son-in-law), Greg Bahnsen, David Chilton, Gary DeMar, and Kenneth Gentry.

Christian Reconstructionism argued for a return to the Mosaic Law as the cornerstone of a new Christian society. This movement has been marked by anti-Semitism and is characterized by its strong anti-Jewish rhetoric. Its leaders have taught that the Church replaced Israel. They argue that Israel's defeat at the hands of the Romans in A.D. 70 and A.D. 135, the destruction of the Temple, and the Holocaust reveal that God has rejected her. Reconstructionist leader Gary DeMar has said:

In destroying Israel, Christ transferred the blessings of the kingdom from Israel to a new people, the Church.[6]

Joining DeMar, the late Christian Reconstructionist leader David Chilton (1951-1997) writes concerning God's so-called judgment upon Israel:

> Because Israel committed the supreme act of covenant breaking when she rejected Christ, Israel herself was rejected by God. The awesome curses pronounced by Jesus, Moses, and the prophets were fulfilled in the terrible destruction of Jerusalem, with the desolation of the Temple and the obliteration of the covenant nation in A.D. 70.[7]

Christian Reconstructionism, by the use of literature, internet websites, debates, and lecture series, has captured an exceptionally strong following among homeschooling Christians, Reformed Christians, and conservative political activists.

Conclusion

Replacement Theology as a biblical viewpoint has not been formed in a vacuum, but has been influenced by history, tragedy, allegorical interpretation, and a number of key theological leaders. Since the second century, Replacement Theology has influenced many Christians. After the Holocaust (1939-45) and the formation of the Jewish state in Israel in 1948, this view began to lose sway among many Christians. However, today this view is on the ascent once again with a new wave of Replacement conferences, books, and lecture series. There is no indication that Replacement Theology will cease to be a dominant view in the near future.

Endnotes

1. Justin, "Dialogue with Trypho", *Anti-Nicene Fathers*, ed. Alexander Roberts, James Donaldson (Peabody, MA:

Hendrickson, 1994), 1:202

2. Origen, "Against Celsus", *Anti-Nicene Fathers,* ed. Alexander Roberts and James Donaldson (Peabody, MA: Hendrickson, 1994), 4:443

3. Harold O. J. Brown, "Christians and Jews--Bound Together," *Christianity Today,* (Aug. 18, 1978): 18

4. Charles Ryrie, *The Basis of the Premillennial Faith,* (Neptune, NJ: Loizeaux Brothers, 1981), p. 46

5. H. T. Lehman, J. Pelikan, ed., *Luther's Works,* vol. 47, (St Louis MO: Concordia, 2002), p. 138-139

6. Gary DeMar, Peter Leithart, *The Reduction of Christianity,* (Ft. Worth, TX: Dominion Press, 1988), p. 213

7. David Chilton, *Paradise Restored,* (Ft. Worth, TX: Dominion Press, 1985), pp. 224-225

Replacement Theology, Israel, and the Church

Distinguishing things that differ is essential in the interpretation of Scripture, and failure to do so yields grave consequences. This is true in all of Scripture. Church history will show that those who were cavalier concerning subtle and important theological differences have brought great harm to the Church. The failure to distinguish between justification and sanctification does damage to the doctrine of grace. The failure to distinguish between law and grace muddies our understanding of salvation by grace through faith alone. So too, the failure to distinguish Israel from the Church will lead to grave consequences. Reluctance to differentiate Israel from the Church has caused some to return to barren liturgical ritual, the unbiblical separation of the clergy and the laity, and even the use of military might to accomplish the will of God. Oliver Cromwell (1599-1658) serves as an illustration of the necessity of discernment in this area.

Oliver Cromwell was a soldier and Puritan statesman. Later, as *Lord Protector*, he ruled Great Britain with an iron fist. His army, called "Ironsides", never lost a battle and was greatly feared. John Bunyan, the author of *Pilgrim's Progress*, served under his command in the English Civil War, and John Milton, the author of *Paradise Lost*, was Cromwell's personal secretary. The "Ironsides" army fought like no other army had since the days of King David in Israel. They would enter battle singing the psalms of David and reciting the *Westminster Confession*. As a father, Cromwell was gentle with his children; but on the battlefield, he was a ruthless warrior. In August of 1649, Cromwell and 12,000 soldiers arrived in Ireland to quell the Catholic rebellion. During the next ten years of bloodshed, it is estimated that about a third of the population was either killed or died of starvation. The majority of Irish Catholics who owned land had it taken away from them and were removed to the barren province of Connacht. Catholic boys and girls were shipped to Barbados and sold to the plantation owners as slaves. The land taken from the Catholics by Cromwell was given to the Protestant soldiers who had participated in the campaign. Before the rebellion in 1641, Catholics owned 59% of the land in Ireland. By the time Cromwell left, the proportion had shrunk to 22%. Many have wondered how Cromwell, as a Christian, could be so devoted to Christ on one hand, and at the same time be so cruel, violent, and ruthless in battle. Concerning this paradox, Christian historian J. H. Merle D'Aubigne writes:

> The great man shared in the error which the Papacy had held during the Middle ages, and which most of the Reformers entertained during the sixteenth and seventeenth centuries. He did not make a sufficient distinction between the old and the new covenants, between the Old and New Testaments. The terrible judgments inflicted by God's command on the unbelieving nations in the times of the judges and kings of Israel appeared to him not only to be authorized, but to necessitate similar judgments. He thought that, like Moses and Joshua, he might slay Balaam with the sword. It may be that he did not follow this out explicitly; but it was with this prejudice and under this impulse that he usually acted. This was wrong. The Jewish theocracy existed no longer; and its rules of conduct had been abolished with it. The precepts which ought to direct the life of a Christian are contained in our Saviour's Sermon on the Mount and in other discourses, as well as in the writings of the Apostles."[1]

Oliver Cromwell acted as he did because he failed to see vital distinctions between Israel and the Church. He was the Church's King David, vanquishing the enemies of the kingdom.

He was England's Joshua fighting the adversaries of God. There are enormous practical consequences at stake when we fail to distinguish differences between Israel of old and the New Testament Church.

The Reformed View Of Israel And The Church

Even today, there are Christians that resist broad distinctions between Israel and the Church. Today, as with their Puritan fore-fathers, Reformed theologians teach that Israel and the Church are not to be distinguished, but are an organic, unified body under the headship of Christ. According to this view, to separate them is to do great theological harm to the teaching of the covenants, the unity of the Church and Israel, and the importance of the law. Reformed theology argues that the term Israel does not represent a national people but the spiritual people of God. Therefore, the members of the Church are considered to be the New Israel. Spiritual Israel of the Old Testament has now entered a new phase of her history and lives on as the Church. The prophecies concerning the nation of Israel are, for the most part, now applied to the Church.

How do Reformed teachers justify their position from the Scriptures? Reformed writers will indeed agree that there are differences between Israel and the Church, but they would counter that there are many unifying links between these two peoples of God. Scriptures such as, *"But he is a Jew which is one inwardly"* (Rom. 2:29); *"For they are not all Israel, which are of Israel"* (Rom. 9:6); and *"the Israel of God"* (Gal. 6:16) are used as support of this position.

Reformed writers teach that natural, national Israel has been set aside by God and will not receive the promises of God; however, believing Israel, the faithful remnant of the Old Testament beginning with Abraham, was the initial phase of what would eventually be called "the Church." It is this spiritual or true Israel, and not national Israel, that is to be identified with the Church.

Reformed author Keith Mathison explains:

We must first note that if "Israel" is defined as natural, national, or unbelieving Israel, then obviously "Israel" is not the Church... If, however, we define "Israel" as true Israel or Old Testament believers, we discover a different relationship. There is an organic, living relationship between Old Testament believers and New Testament believers. They are one body joined together under one head, the Lord Jesus Christ.[2]

Replacement theologian Louis Berkhof writes in his *Systematic Theology:*

The Church existed in the old dispensation as well as in the new and was essentially the same in both.[3]

An Examination Of The Reformed View

Is it indeed true that Scripture considers only believing Israel to be the true Israel? Does Scripture teach that only those of believing Israel are the true possessors of the covenant promises? Is this true Israel of the Old Testament the beginning of what is now the New Testament Church? Let us examine this Reformed view in light of the Word of God. All sincere students of Scripture will admit that there are similarities between Israel and the Church. But at the same time, they will also agree that there are great differences. Often, the differences can be the doors that open to us important doctrinal truth. So it is in the study of God's plan for Israel. The careful study of Scripture reveals that God has a plan for Israel, and this plan involves both the believing and the unbelieving parts of the nation. Yes, God has always had a remnant of believers in Israel throughout history (Rom. 11), but it must also be said that He has not cast away the unbelieving in Israel. They are both part of His divine plan.

How does Scripture define the composition of what is called Israel? Notice what Peter states while preaching to the Jews near Solomon's porch in Acts chapter three:

"I know that ye through ignorance did it... Ye are the
children of the prophets, and of the covenant which God
made with our fathers, saying unto Abraham, 'And in
thy seed shall all the kindreds of the earth be blessed'"
(Acts 3:17, 25).

Peter begins by saying you — the unbelieving Jewish people — although through ignorance, are responsible for the death of Christ. He then turns to the subject of who the possessors of the promises of the covenant are. Who is the "seed" through which all the nations would be blessed? Peter unequivocally states that it is those who crucified Christ, unbelieving Israel, who are possessors of the covenant; these are "Israel."

This leads us to another consideration. Who among the Jewish people is "elect Israel" — national Israel or believing Israel? Paul writes and explains to the Romans that it is unbelieving Israel, the "enemies of the gospel" who are elect. Paul writes in Romans chapter eleven:

"As concerning the gospel, they are enemies for your sakes;
but as touching the election, they are beloved for the fath-
ers' sakes. For the gifts and calling of God are without
repentance" (Rom. 11:28-29).

God has not cast off the unbelieving in Israel. They are an integral part of God's divine plan for Israel. So it again is both believing and unbelieving who are considered elect Israel.

Dispensational View Of Israel And The Church

Dispensationalists view the relationship between Israel and the Church very differently than Reformed teachers do. Dispensationalists maintain that a consistent interpretation of Scripture necessitates a distinction between Israel and the Church. While there is indeed a connection between the Church and the saved within Israel, there are, nevertheless, varied and important differences. Some dispensationalists, such as Lewis Sperry Chafer, have detailed as many as twenty-four important theological differences. Other dispensationalists have argued for fewer, but nonetheless important, differences.

The Church	Israel
1. The Church is a mystery.	1. Israel is never spoken of as a mystery
2. The Church began at Pentecost when the Holy Spirit formed the disciples into the body of Christ.	2. The nation of Israel began with the call of Abraham (Gen. 12).
3. Christ is the head of the Church.	3. Abraham was the head of Israel.
4. Membership in the Church is by spiritual new birth	4. Membership in the nation of Israel was by natural birth.
5. The Church is a priesthood; each member is a believer priest.	5. Israel had a priesthood, the sons of Aaron.

6. Jew and Gentile would form a new body, which the Bible calls "one new man." This idea was revolutionary; the Jewish people accepted Gentiles who became proselytes of Judaism. But now a Jew and Gentile would be on equal footing in the same body through the cross of Christ.	6. Israel considered Gentiles to be unfit for the blessings of God. They would have nothing to do with them. "They were aliens from the commonwealth of Israel...having no hope and without God in the world" (Eph. 2:12)
7. At the Rapture, the Church will be taken to heaven, and after the Tribulation period, return with Christ to reign with Him on the earth.	7. Redeemed Israel will live on earth but not reign with Him during the 1,000 years.
8. The citizenship of the Church is in heaven. "For our citizenship is in heaven; from whence we look for the Saviour..." (Phil. 3:20).	8. The citizenship of Israel was earthly. Their nation was the land of Israel with Jerusalem as its capital.

God's Program For Israel

Israel was chosen by God to be a special people for Himself (Deut. 7:6). The Jews are God's vessel to reveal His will to mankind and to be the ethnic line from which the Lord Jesus Christ would descend. God made it clear that this choice of Israel would be eternal. Jeremiah wrote that Israel would continue as a nation as long as the sun, moon, and stars endure (Jer. 31:35-37). Scripture lays well-placed emphasis upon this eternal relationship with Israel when God spoke of giving *"all the land of Canaan"* as an everlasting possession (Gen. 17:8). Possession, however, does not mean *occupancy*, for Israel has been removed from the land (Deut. 28) at least three times in biblical history. Furthermore, God forewarned Israel of her dispersions from the land and her promised restoration (Deut. 30:1-6).

In addition to Israel's everlasting existence and possession of the land, God has promised to Israel an everlasting kingdom. God promised to David and his descendants that they would have a kingdom that would be forever (2 Sam. 7:12-14). God made it clear that if they departed from His ways, they would be chastised by the nations, but He would never remove the kingdom from David's family line as He did from Saul. As the years passed, the latter Old Testament prophets predicted that God would re-gather Israel from the ends of the earth, and Christ would then reign and rule on earth from Jerusalem (Zech. 14:9, Hab. 2:14). In the New Testament, we find that God continues to be occupied with Israel through His Son. In the four gospels, the Lord Jesus Christ preached, ministered, and served almost exclusively to those from the nation of Israel. However, the apostle John, at the outset of his gospel, tells us solemnly *"He came to His own and His own received Him not"* (John 1:11). The Lord had come to the Jews to offer them a King and a kingdom. But the nation did not receive her king; instead, they crucified the Lord of glory. The Lord Jesus in His sovereignty knew full well that the nation would reject this offer; nevertheless, this offer was sincere and bona fide.

God's Program For The Church

As we open the first pages of the book of Acts, we see God now doing something new. We do not read much of Israel, but rather, now we read of a new body, *the Church*. God has temporarily set aside Israel and has taken up the Church to accomplish

His purposes. In the Old Testament, Israel was clearly distinct from the Gentile nations. However, as one moves into the New Testament, Israel is not only distinct from the Gentiles, but now she is also distinct from the Church of God. The New Testament divides all mankind into three categories: Israel, the Gentiles, and the Church of God. Paul writes, *"Give no offense, either to the Jews or to the Gentiles or to the Church of God* (1 Cor. 10:32). Earlier in the New Testament, these three groups of humanity are mentioned in one passage, Acts 15:14-17: (1) The Church — *"...God at the first did visit the Gentiles to **take out of them a people for His name**"* (Acts 15:14). (2) Israel — *"...After this I will return and will rebuild the tabernacle of David, which has fallen down; I will rebuild the ruins, and I will set it up"* (Acts 15:16). (3) The Gentiles — *"So that the rest of mankind may seek the Lord, even all **the Gentiles** who are called by My name, says the Lord who does all these things"* (Acts 15:17). Moreover, Paul's letters emphasize the identity of these groups by using imagery from the rite of circumcision. He calls the Church, *"the circumcision made without hands"* (Col. 2:11); Israel, *"the circumcision"* (Eph. 2:11); and the Gentiles, *"uncircumcision"* (Eph. 2:11).

However, in the New Testament the group with which God is most occupied is the Church. The Church is called by various titles in the New Testament, but the most common and important title is the "body." Interestingly, Israel is never called "the body" in the Old or New Testaments. Paul writes that God, before the foundation of the world, had planned that both Jew and Gentile would come together to form a new body, which he calls *"one new man."* The Church, as a body, is a mystery (Eph. 3:4); that which was not revealed in the Old Testament is now revealed in the New Testament. This idea was revolutionary; the Jewish people accepted Gentiles who became proselytes of Judaism. But for a Jew and Gentile to be on equal footing in the same body through the cross of Jesus Christ was unimaginable. This was never true of Israel. However, the Church is much more than simply a body; it is the Body of Christ, united to her risen Head in heaven. *"God hath raised us up together and made us to sit together in heavenly places in Christ Jesus."* The Lord, in stressing this point, said,

"Ye are not of the world even as I am not of the world" (John 17:14). Therefore, we may say that the Church is heaven-centered, while Israel was for the most part earth-centered. Israel has an earthly calling but a heavenly hope (Heb. 11:16), whereas the Church has a heavenly calling and a heavenly hope.

God is now fulfilling His purposes by the Church. God is not using the Church to "Christianize" the world, nor to fight the world, nor to isolate itself from the world, but to take out a people for His name from the world. This high position of the Church is seen in its formation. As a result of the baptism of the Holy Spirit, which formed the body of Christ, the Church, each believer is now *"in Christ."* The Pauline term *"in Christ"* is a theological phrase that teaches that the believer is placed in spiritual union with Christ. *"One who joins himself to the Lord is one spirit with Him"* (1 Cor. 6:17, NASB). The believer is identified with Him in His death, burial, and resurrection unto *"newness of life."* Christ's riches are our riches, His power is our power, His resources are our resources, and His position is our position. To be *"in Christ"* is to share in the very life of God through Jesus Christ (Eph. 1:3). Paul continues detailing the high position of the New Testament Church in Ephesians by speaking of the indwelling ministry of the Holy Spirit. As a result of this baptism of the Holy Spirit, the indwelling presence of the Holy Spirit is promised to each believer (Eph. 1:13). This indwelling of the Holy Spirit as a seal and earnest of God is permanent, despite the sinful deeds of the believer that grieve the Holy Spirit. In the upper room, the Lord Jesus said, *"...the Father, He shall give you another Comforter, that He may abide with you forever"* (John 14:16).

Conclusion

Old Testament Israel did not know the blessings of being *"in Christ"* or of the permanent indwelling of the Holy Spirit. God's program with the Church is different than His program with Israel. God has designed Israel to have a different role and purpose than the Church. These two programs, along with God's programs for angels and the nations, form God's one unique plan for the ages. This plan does not slight one group over the other, but in the sovereignty and wisdom of God, this plan brings to the Lord Jesus Christ the highest glory.

Endnotes

1. J. H. Merle D'Aubigne, *The Protector: A Vindication*, (New York, NY: Robert Carter, 1947), p. 106-107

2. Keith Mathison, *Dispensationalism: Wrongly Dividing the People of God*, (Phillipsburg, NJ: P & R Publishing, 1995), p. 38, 39

3. Louis Berkhof, *Systematic Theology*, (Grand Rapids, MI: Eerdmans,1941), p. 571

Replacement Theology and Important Bible Texts

Modern Dispensational leaders have taught for 150 years that God is not yet finished with Israel. They take seriously the promises and the covenants given by God to Israel in the Old Testament. They still believe the words of the apostle Paul, who asks rhetorically, *"Has God cast away His people?"* (Rom. 11:1). The answer is, of course, "God forbid!" However, not all Christians have the same view regarding Israel. Replacement leaders disagree with the view that Israel is still the people of God. They reject the idea that there is still a future hope for the nation of Israel in the plan of God. They teach that the Church has replaced Israel and that the promises to Israel in the Old Testament are now fulfilled in the Church. Richard Mouw, president of Fuller Seminary, in California, illustrates this view when he relates his experience in writing a paper on Romans chapter eleven:

> I chose to write on Romans 11, where the apostle Paul discusses the theological status of the Jews since the coming of Christ. I eagerly set about to complete the assignment, reading commentators who set forth a variety of interpretations. I also worked through the chapter in the Greek language, reading it over many times... I was studying in a Reformed Seminary, and I was eager to demonstrate that the promises associated with God's old covenant with ethnic Israel have now been transferred to the church of Jesus Christ, the new people of the covenant. But I did not know how to make the case confidently, so I never wrote the paper.[1]

Replacement writers chide Dispensational leaders for being too supportive of Israel and urge them to consider the political viewpoints of Arab nations and the Palestinians within Israel's borders. Again, we turn to Richard Mouw, when he writes:

> I find Dispensationalism to be especially unhelpful—even an obstacle at times that stands in the way of clear thinking about the church's mission. I am especially disturbed by what I see as a refusal on the part of many Dispensationalists to criticize the policies of Israeli governments... they (Dispensationalists) are often so caught up in an enthusiasm for Bible prophecy scenarios that they take it as obligatory to support Israel no matter what.[2]

Dispensationalists are unapologetic in siding with God concerning the Jewish nation. On one hand, they understand that Israel today is a secular nation; on the other hand, they cannot deny that God has brought the nation back into its land, and that the events unfolding in the Middle East merely foreshadow God's future restoration of the nation and the fulfillment of His promises.

Replacement Christians point to a handful of Bible texts in support of their point of view. We will examine their interpretations in the light of the entire Word of God. The Bible must be the foundation that leads us to our doctrine. Doctrine must not be based upon personal bias and opinions. The question Replacement Christians wrestle with is this: Does God have a future plan for the nation of Israel? They will agree that believing Jewish Christians are included in God's plans, but not the unbelieving part of the nation of Israel. The Bible texts and passages we will examine are those that touch on this question.

Romans 9:6 - *"To Whom Pertain...the Covenants..."*

To whom does the term "Israel" apply? Is it unbelieving Israel, national Israel, or the "New Israel"— the Church? The

New Testament answers this very question when Paul, writing to the Romans, states:

> "...who are the Israelites, to whom pertaineth the adoption, and the glory, and the covenants, and the giving of the law, and the service of God, and the promises; whose are the fathers and of whom, as concerning the flesh, Christ came, who is over all, God blessed forever. Amen" (Rom. 9:4-5).

In these verses Paul answers two questions. Firstly, who is Israel? Secondly, to whom belong the promises of God? We should, first of all, note that the book of Romans was written about A.D. 60, many years after the formation of the Church; yet Paul states that the adoption, the covenants, and the promises still are the possession of Israel. Paul uses the present tense throughout this verse to first define an "Israelite", and then to show who possesses the promises of God. He writes, "*Who are the Israelites...to who pertaineth adoption, service to God... whose are the fathers...*" If the promises of God to Old Testament Israel now applied to the Church, one would expect that after sixty years, New Testament writers would clearly set forth this fact in the Word of God. It seems, however, that the promises to Israel still apply to Israel, and the definition of "Israel" has not changed.

Let none misunderstand. Scripture does not teach that literal, national Israel comes into rich blessing from God simply because they are Jews. Jesus said to the Jews, "*Think not to say within yourselves, 'We have Abraham as our father': For I say unto you that God is able of these stones to raise up children of Abraham*" (Matt. 3:9)..."*If you were Abraham's children, you would do the works of Abraham*" (John 8:39). God has never given His promises to Israel merely because they were Israelites after the flesh. The promises of God, which will be fulfilled in the coming kingdom, are only for those who through faith have come to Christ. When and how will this take place? National Israel and believing Israel will become one and will enter into the millennial promises of God at the appearing of Christ, when in the words of Paul, "*So all Israel shall be saved: as it is written,*

'There shall come a Deliverer and He shall turn away ungodliness from Jacob'" (Rom. 11:26 KJV).

German theologian Erich Sauer (1898-1952) explains:

> Through the conversion of the Jews at the appearing of Messiah, the faith of the little remnant extends to the whole body. The literal Israel has thus become spiritual Israel. Abraham's descendants according to the flesh have by conversion and regeneration become true sons of the patriarch, and thus, at the same time, Israel according to the spirit (Gal. 3:9). Thenceforth, the national is identical with the spiritual. The remnant has become the whole people, and the saved national people are at the same time both literal descendants of Abraham and also his spiritual seed.[3]

Romans 11:1 - *"Hath God Cast Away His People?"*

Another question with which Replacement Christians grapple is whether God has, once and for all, terminated His relationship with Israel. Is there a future for Israel? Is God then finished with Israel? Paul answers this question in Romans chapter 11, writing, *"I say then, Hath God cast away His people? God forbid!"* (Rom. 11:1). God has not set aside the people of Israel forever. He has not given the promises to Israel in the Old Testament to the Church. God's faithfulness to Israel will *"endure unto all generations."*

The question needs to be addressed: To *whom* is Paul referring when he speaks of *"His people"*? Undoubtedly, he is not speaking concerning the church; if the church were his focus, he certainly would have made this clear. It would be foolish to conclude he was speaking to Jewish believers within Israel. Why would Paul say *"Hath God cast away His people?"* if these Jews within Israel were believers? The only reasonable viewpoint is that Paul is speaking about unbelieving Israel who has rejected the Lord Jesus Christ.

This becomes all the more clear when we look at the last verse of the preceding chapter: *"...A disobedient and gainsaying people"* (Romans 10:21). God is speaking of national Israel. So Paul takes up the question and faces it squarely, *"Hath God cast away his people?"* The answer that is given in Romans 11 is absolutely NO. Paul responds to this question with a three-fold answer:

1. Paul, using himself as an example, asserts that there are presently many Jews that are saved, which proves God has not cast them off.

2. There will be a future salvation of thousands of Jewish people: *"What shall the receiving of them be but life from the dead"*(11:15)? Paul may be thinking of Ezekiel 37 and the Valley of Dry Bones.

3. There will be a final salvation and *"All Israel shall be saved"* (vv. 26-27). Has God cast off His people?

Dr. Alva McClain, the former president of Grace Theological Seminary, with insight answers this question:

> There is a school of thought in Christendom that says that in the church God has fulfilled everything in the Old Testament and there is no future for the Jews as a nation. The right view is, that God has set Israel aside for an age, and at some future time (the next age) God will fulfill to the letter every promise He has made to Israel as a nation."[4]

Romans 11:26 - *"...And All Israel Shall Be Saved"*

During the time of the tribulation, following the rapture of the Church, Israel will experience a spiritual awakening. As the tribulation nears its end, there will be a great movement of the Spirit of God, and the Scripture teaches that all Israel will be saved. Paul writes in Romans, *"And so all Israel shall be saved; as it is written, 'There shall come out of Zion the Deliverer, and He shall turn away ungodliness from Jacob'"* (Rom. 11:26). The question has been raised: Will every individual Jew be saved?

The spiritual, judicial hardening of Israel was neither final nor total, for the time will come when the day of grace for Gentiles will give way to the time of restoration for the Jewish people. While Israel's veil of blindness concerning her Messiah will be removed following the rapture, this does not mean all of Israel will be saved right away. Jews will be converted throughout the tribulation period, but the entire elect remnant will not be saved until Christ returns to earth as King of Kings and Lord of Lords.

When Paul says that all Israel shall be saved, we must understand that he means all believing Israel. The beloved Bible expositor Harry Ironside (1876-1951) writes:

> We are not to understand by the term "all Israel" everyone of Israel's blood, for we have already learned that "they are not all Israel who are of Israel, but the children of promise are counted for the seed." So the remnant will be the true Israel in that glorious day when, "There shall come out of Zion the Deliverer, and He shall turn away ungodliness from Jacob," for God has said: "This is My covenant unto them when I shall take away their sins."[5]

The God of Abraham, Isaac, and Jacob will do a wonderful, supernatural work in the nation of Israel during the tribulation period. Thousands upon thousands of Jewish people will say concerning the Messiah, *"Blessed is He who comes in the name of the Lord."* This is what Isaiah referred to when he spoke of the Deliverer coming to Zion and turning ungodliness away from Jacob (Isaiah 59:20).

Reformed writer Charles Hodge (1797-1878) provides further insight when he comments on Romans 11:26:

> Israel, here, from the context, must mean the Jewish people, and all Israel, the whole nation. The Jews, as a people, are not rejected; as a people, they are to be

restored. As their rejection, although national, did not include the rejection of every individual, so their restoration, although in like manner national, need not be assumed to include the salvation of every individual Jew. Pas Israel ("All Israel") is not therefore to be understood to mean all the true people of God (the Church) as Augustine, Calvin, and many others explain it; nor all the elect Jews, i.e., all that part of the nation which constitutes the "remnant according to the election of grace;" but the whole nation, as a nation.[6]

Hodge's comments are important, firstly, because he rejects the standing Reformed view of Replacement Theology; and secondly, because he highlights the powerful work of God in the hearts of the Jewish nation at the end of the tribulation. Concerning the first point, Hodge, a Reformed theologian, dismisses the view of Calvin and his followers, who insist that "Israel" must be reinterpreted as the "true people of God, the Church". He repudiates the view that God is finished with Israel, affirming that Israel must be interpreted as the literal nation of Israel. As to the second point, he concludes that although not every individual Jew will be saved, nevertheless, God will work in a special way, resulting in the salvation of the greater part of the Jewish nation. Bible commentator Warren Wiersbe joins him when he writes:

> There are those who interpret this as meaning salvation to individuals through the gospel, but it is my conviction that the prophet has national conversion in mind. "All Israel shall be saved" does not mean every Jew that has ever lived will be converted, but the Jews living when the Redeemer returns will see Him, receive Him, and be saved…there are too many details in these Old Testament prophecies of a national restoration for us to spiritualize and apply them to the Church.[7]

The Old Testament prophets frequently speak of this

remarkable work of salvation. Joel writes, *"And it shall come to pass that I will pour out My Spirit upon all flesh...and it shall come to pass whosoever shall call upon the name of the Lord shall be delivered"* (Joel 2:28-32). Ezekiel states, *"A new heart also will I give you and a new spirit will I put in you, and I will take away the stony heart out of your flesh, and I will give you a heart of flesh. And I will put My Spirit within you and cause you to walk in My statutes, and you shall keep My judgments and do them"* (Ezek. 36:26-27). Ezekiel continues in chapter 37, where he speaks of the nation of Israel as the valley of dry bones, a spiritually dead nation. These bones, he states, are lifeless— *"very dry"* and spiritually dead. Ezekiel explains that through the preaching of the Word (v. 4) and the divine breath of the Spirit, God will cause these bones to live, saying *"...(I) shall put My Spirit in you, and ye shall live, and I will place you in your own land..."* (37:14). This powerful work of God in Israel, near the end of the tribulation period, will result in thousands turning to God in faith, and the greater part of Israel will be saved. God has not cast off His people; they are, indeed, the "apple of His eye" and He will one day say, *"...they which were not My people, 'Thou art My people'; and they shall say 'Thou art my God'"* (Hosea 2:23).

More Debated Passages

There are a number of passages in the Bible that have caused confusion to Christians.

Matthew 24:22

The first of these passages is Matthew 24, which is also called the Olivet Discourse. The latter section of this passage concerns Israel, not the church. It describes conditions prior to the second coming of Christ to earth to reign as King. We read, *"but for the elect's sake those days shall be shortened"* (Matt. 24:22). This verse has troubled some who have interpreted the reference to the *"elect"* in this verse as referring to the Church. However, Israel is also the elect of God. In fact, Israel is mentioned more frequently throughout Scripture as "the elect" or "chosen" than is the Church (Deut. 7:6, Ps. 135:4, Isa. 41:8-9).

To further support the fact that this section is referring to Israel, note the reference to the Sabbath, *"And pray that your flight may not be...on the Sabbath;"* and the reference to the land of Israel, *"Then let those who are in Judea flee to the mountains."* This passage is speaking about the Lord Jesus Christ returning to the earth at His second coming, to rule and reign from Jerusalem to close out the Great Tribulation and to usher in the millennium.

Acts 7:38

In the King James Version of Acts 7:38, Israel is called *"the church in the wilderness."* But we must realize that the word translated *"church"* (*ecclesia*) simply means an assembly or company of people. The NASB rendering of "congregation," a word still favored in Jewish circles today, better captures this truth. The same word is used to describe an angry mob in Ephesus (Acts. 19:32).

Galatians 6:16

The verse used most frequently by Reformed leaders to teach Replacement Theology is Galatians 6:16. Paul writes, *"And as many as walk according to this rule, peace and mercy be upon them and upon the Israel of God."* In this view, the expression *"Israel of God"* is used to argue that all believers in the Church today form the "New Israel," the *"Israel of God."* We believe this is a misunderstanding. When Paul says *"peace be on them,"* he is referring to all believers. But in the words *"Israel of God,"* Paul singles out those believers of Jewish birth who walk according to the rule of the new creation (v. 15), not according to the rule of law. Bible teacher David Levy, in his commentary on Galatians, writes:

> Some scholars believe that Paul's reference to the *"Israel of God"* applies to all true believers—Jews and Gentiles—who make up the Church. This cannot be the correct interpretation for a number of reasons. First, the phrase *"and upon the Israel of God"* is an afterthought to the general benediction and shows

Paul's desire for Jewish people who embrace the gospel of Christ to receive God's peace and mercy, referring to the true remnant within Israel. This passage recognizes the true Jewish believers within the church...[8]

Endnotes

1. Richard Mouw, "The Chosen People Puzzle", *Christianity Today*, March 5, 2001, p. 73

2. Richard Mouw, "The Chosen People Puzzle", *Christianity Today*, March 5, 2001, p. 74

3. Erich Sauer, *Eternity to Eternity*, (Grand Rapids, MI : Eerdmans, 1979), p. 160-161

4. Alva McClain, *Romans: The Gospel of God's Grace*, (Winona Lake, IN: BHM, 1973), p. 196

5. Harry A. Ironside, *Romans*, (New York, NY: Loizeaux, 1976), p. 142-143

6. Charles Hodge, *Romans*, (Grand Rapids, MI : Eerdmans, 1964), p. 374

7. Warren Wiersbe, *Romans, Bible Exposition Commentary, vol. 1*, (Wheaton, IL: Victor, 1989), p. 552

8. David Levy, *Guarding the Gospel of Grace*, (Bellmawr, NJ: Friends of Israel, 1997), p. 132

The New Covenant and Replacement Theology

The institution of the New Covenant powerfully unfolds the depth of God's faithfulness and the integrity of His promises. This unconditional agreement was made with Israel because they had broken the terms of the earlier Mosaic covenant. This (new) covenant would be rooted in God›s faithfulness rather than Israel›s obedience. It points to a future day, when God will gather Israel out of all the nations and bring them into their own land, giving them a new heart and a new spirit (Ezek. 36:28). He will own them as His covenant people - *"a nation born in a day."* He will merge the two parts of divided Israel into one nation under one sovereign King, and set His sanctuary in the midst of them forever (Ezek. 37:15).

The authority of the New Covenant is anchored upon the blood of Christ, the Mediator of the covenant (Heb. 8:13). Because of this fact, Christ is called by the writer of the book of Hebrews to be now the Mediator of the New Covenant, *"He is the mediator of a better covenant"* (Heb. 8:6). The Lord's Supper demonstrates this — *"This cup is the New Covenant in My blood which is shed for you"* (Luke 22:19). As Christians, we are identified with the glorious Mediator and enjoy the spiritual privileges and blessings of the New Covenant, but it is essentially a covenant with Israel. Its final consummation awaits the time when *"the Deliverer will come out of Zion, and...turn away ungodliness from Jacob"* (Rom. 11:25). Afterwards, this covenant will be fully realized by Israel in the millennial age.

Reformed Theology And Dispensationalism

However, Reformed-Replacement teachers see this dispensational understanding of the New Covenant as a weak link in Dispensational theology. Reformed literature seeks at every turn to attack traditional dispensational teaching concerning the New Covenant. A leading Replacement theologian, Professor Keith Mathison, writes:

> The New Covenant is perhaps the clearest example of a promise made to national Israel that is now being fulfilled in and by the church. Dispensationalists have consistently taught that the church cannot fulfill the new covenant of Jeremiah 31…Dispensationalists insist that the church cannot fulfill the New Covenant because such a fulfillment would undermine the doctrine of premillennialism…[1]

Current Reformed-Replacement Theology teaches that the church now fulfills the provisions of the New Covenant. The Reformed view has been adopted by a growing number of Charismatic leaders to buttress their view for miracles and healing during this age. They teach that since Christ is presently reigning as the covenantal King, the church should experience the supernatural blessings of the New Covenant today. This view has been espoused by many past and present Charismatic leaders such as Jack Hayford, John Wimber, Peter C. Wagner, and others. This view teaches that Christ, as the Mediator of the New Covenant is now seated on His millennial throne in heaven. From this center of His kingdom authority, miracles, physical healing, and power over demons will flow down to His people on earth in an unprecedented way. Elements of this "Kingdom Authority" teaching have even found their way into contemporary praise music. Jack Hayford, a Charismatic pastor and musician from Van Nuys, California, in the lyrics to his song "Majesty" writes: "Majesty, kingdom authority flow from His throne unto His own, His anthem raise." This teaching is inevitable when the Reformed view of the New Covenant is carried to its logical conclusion.

A Problem Passage: Hebrews 8:6

Replacement theologians are quick to point to Hebrews chapter eight as support for their view that the provisions of the New Covenant are fulfilled in the church. In Hebrews chapter eight we read, *"...by how much also He is the Mediator of a better covenant, which was established upon better promises"* (Heb. 8:6). Calvinistic writers place emphasis on the phrase *"He is the Mediator of a better covenant."* They argue that Christ presently is the Mediator of the terms of the New Covenant. They contend that since Christ is now the Mediator of the New Covenant, then the Covenant is now fulfilled by the Church, and not by Israel in a future millennial kingdom. They teach that Israel has no future millennial hope, nor should they expect any future fulfillment of the New Covenant. Some Reformed leaders seem to believe that this viewpoint is the most convincing interpretation of this verse. Reformed theologian Keith Mathison, writes:

> Hebrews 8:6-13 tells us that Jesus is the Mediator of the New Covenant now. Hebrews teaches repeatedly that the old covenant has been abolished and that the New Covenant has been inaugurated by Jesus Christ through the shedding of His blood. [2]

The Two-Fold Structure Of The New Covenant

There is an important theological distinction between inauguration and institution. *Inauguration* indicates the fulfilling of the provisions of the covenant, whereas *institution* refers to the setting forth of the terms of the covenant. Has the New Covenant been partially inaugurated? Yes, for we are told in Hebrews 8 that Christ is the Mediator of the covenant; but must we then conclude that the Church now replaces Israel in fulfilling all the provisions of the New Covenant? How have Dispensational writers answered this question? Dispensationalism offers a reasonable explanation to the question of how Christ is presently the Mediator of the New Covenant, but the New Covenant is not yet completely fulfilled in the church. In defense of their position, many Dispensational writers point to the two-level structure of the four major biblical covenants. In each these, the covenant was first instituted, and then many years later, some or all of the covenant's provisions were *fulfilled*. In the Abrahamic Covenant, God unconditionally promised a seed (son) to Abraham and Sarah; however it was not until twenty-five years later that that provision of the covenant was fulfilled. In the Davidic Covenant, one of the terms of this unconditional covenant was that from David's seed One would come who would *"build a house for My name"* (2 Sam. 7:13). This would not take place until the reign of Solomon many years later. God's pattern for His covenants is that a covenant is first introduced, and then many years later, the provisions of the covenant are fulfilled. This is also the pattern of the New Covenant. The New Covenant was introduced by the Mediator, the Lord Jesus Christ, and it was sealed by our Lord when His blood was shed on the cross of Calvary. The provisions of the covenant were offered to the nation of Israel after the resurrection of Christ, but were rejected. Nevertheless, the terms of the covenant will be fulfilled in the nation of Israel during the millennial reign of the Lord Jesus Christ.

Elliot Johnson, a professor of New Testament at Dallas Theological Seminary, explains:

> The distinction between the institution and the fulfillment of a covenant must be clarified further. To institute a promissory covenant is to introduce provisions of the agreement that are now available to be received. To inaugurate fulfillment is to keep all of the provisions of the agreement. The new covenant was instituted only after the death of Christ, the Mediator of the covenant; then He and the provisions of the covenant were offered to the nation, following His resurrection and ascension. Some of the provisions were then made available as given to the remnant gathered in Jerusalem for Pentecost. The new covenant will be inaugurated in fulfillment when Israel as a nation will accomplish her national destiny.[3]

Theologian Dr. Dwight Pentecost, an adjunct professor at Dallas Theological Seminary, adds:

> There is a marked and critical difference between the institution of the covenant and the realization of its benefits. By Christ's death, Christ laid the foundation for Israel's new covenant—but its benefits will not be received by Israel until the second advent of Messiah. [4]

The New Covenant And Israel

The New and Old Testaments provide support for the idea that national Israel will still inherit the spiritual and temporal provisions of the New Covenant. If this is true, then it is a powerful argument against the view that the church replaces Israel and inherits all of the provisions of the New Covenant. As we look more closely at this subject, the Holy Scriptures must be our only standard and guide. There are two main categories into which the biblical evidence can be arranged: 1) The integrity of God's promises to Israel, and 2) a look at both the national and material promises to Israel.

The Integrity Of God's Promises To National Israel

The Scriptures teach that God must be absolutely faithful to His Word. In the New Covenant, He has unconditionally bound Himself to be faithful to its provisions and terms. In Jeremiah 31 and in Hebrews 8 (where the terms of the New Covenant are discussed), no less than five times does God use the phrase "I will" to express His loyalty to the terms of the New Covenant. This is essential, for God's integrity, His faithfulness, and the veracity of His character are at stake. The psalmist comforts himself in God's faithfulness when he reminds us, "*My covenant I will not break, nor alter the word that has gone out of My lips*" (Ps. 89:34). In the New Testament, sixty years after the birth of

Christ, the apostle Paul in the book of Romans tells us that Israel still possesses the provisions contained in the covenants. Paul writes, *"Who are Israelites; to whom pertain the adoption, and the glory, and the covenants..."* (Romans 9:4). The use of the present tense by Paul in this verse is very important: *"to whom pertain... the covenants."* The present tense indicates that God has never wavered in His promises made to Israel.

National And Material Promises

Closely associated with the fact that God must be faithful to His promises, is the uniqueness of the covenant provisions to Israel. God has made both spiritual and material promises to Israel. Today, the Church enjoys some of the spiritual blessings of the New Covenant by virtue of the death of the Lord Jesus Christ. However, in a careful study of the New Covenant, it soon becomes obvious that many of its spiritual and material provisions can only be fulfilled by national Israel in the future millennium. By their very nature, it is impossible for these promises to be fulfilled today in the Church. Allow us to look at just a few of them. The prophet Ezekiel, in chapter 34, begins to speak of some of the blessings of the New Covenant. In this chapter, he calls it a *"covenant of peace"* (v. 25) and states that Israel will be *"His people and He will be their God,"* a provision of the New Covenant detailed in Jeremiah 31 and Hebrews 8.

Clearly the context of this passage is that these are blessings, which flow out of God's New Covenant relationship to the nation of Israel. Notice some of the provisions:

1. Wild animals will be removed from out of the land so that the inhabitants may sleep in safety in the fields and woods (v. 25).

2. There will be a supernaturally abundant harvest of farm crops and other agriculture from the land (v. 27).

3. Israel will not receive any threats and insults from other nations (Ezekiel 34: 28-29).

All of these provisions mentioned by Ezekiel have not taken place today either in the Church or in the land of Israel; they are provisions of the New Covenant that will be fulfilled in the future.

Additionally, in Jeremiah 31:34, the prophet mentions that *"they shall teach no more every man his neighbor and every man his brother, saying, 'Know the Lord': for they shall know Me from the least of them unto the greatest of them."* This is one of the spiritual provisions in the New Covenant that is certainly reserved for the future. Clearly, this is not true today, even in the Church. Instead of seeing a growing knowledge of the things of God, we are presently seeing a sharp decline in the knowledge of the Lord and of spiritual things.

Conclusion

The New Covenant is expressly promised to both the house of Israel and the house of Judah. It is a better covenant than the one God made with Israel at Mount Sinai, as it provides for the future salvation of the nation and endows the people with the ability to walk in God's laws and statutes (Heb. 8:10). Under these conditions, the nation of Israel will be able to safely dwell in her own land under the shelter of the Lord Jesus Christ, the King of the Jews. The Church, on the other hand, is the Body and espoused Bride of Christ. As such, she bears witness on earth to the fact that Christ, as Mediator of the New Covenant, has shed His blood for the remission of sins.

Endnotes

1. Keith Mathison, *Rightly Dividing the People of God?*, (Phillipsburg, PA: P & R Publishing, 1995), p. 28

2. Ibid., p. 29

3. Elliot Johnson, *Contemporary Dispensationalism*, (Grand Rapids, MI: Kregel, 1999), p. 146

4. Dwight Pentecost, *Thy Kingdom Come*, (Grand Rapids, MI: Kregel, 1995), p. 173

Replacement Theology and Anti-Semitism

David Roberts (1796-1864), a Scottish-born artist, rose from poverty to become one of the most popular painters of the nineteenth century. He became an active member of Britain's Royal Academy. He traveled extensively in the Middle East in the 1840s, creating well over 250 paintings and drawings, which beautifully depicted majestic and historic scenes of this ancient land. Robert's pictures of the Holy Land were his most famous; they catapulted him to his first great success as an artist. His oil painting titled *The Siege and Destruction of Jerusalem by the Romans Under the Command of Titus, A.D. 70* was considered his finest work. The original, painted in 1849, measured an incredible 7 by 12 feet. In order to ensure the greatest possible accuracy in this particular painting, Roberts called upon the writings of Jewish historian Flavius Josephus, an eyewitness to the Roman siege and the destruction of Jerusalem.

The destruction of Jerusalem by the Romans under Titus is one of the greatest calamities in all history. Over one million Jews were killed and 97,000 others were taken to be slaves in the Roman Empire. Amazingly, the current Replacement Theology movement has adopted Robert's painting of the destruction of Jerusalem as a symbol of their movement. The lithograph of this painting is sold by Replacement publishing houses, and its image is found on the letterhead of many Replacement organizations. The use of this artist's rendering of the smoldering ashes of Jerusalem in A.D. 70 strikes many as though Replacement Christians rejoice in the destruction of the Holy City and the agony of the nation of Israel. This apparent pleasure derived from the suffering of the Jewish people is not an isolated event. The history of Replacement Theology has unfortunately been linked to the history of anti-Semitism from the second century onward.

Anti-Semitism Defined

What is anti-Semitism? Anti-Semitism is defined as "suspicion of, hatred toward, or discrimination against Jews for reasons connected to their Jewish heritage." A person who holds such views is called an "anti-Semite". Anti-Semitism may be manifested in many ways, ranging from expressions of hatred toward or discrimination against individual Jews, to organized violent attacks by mobs or even state police, to full-blown military attacks on entire Jewish communities. Extreme instances of persecution include the First Crusade of 1096, the expulsion of Jews from England in 1290, the Spanish Inquisition, the expulsion of Jews from Spain in 1492 and from Portugal in 1497, various pogroms, and the Holocaust by Nazi Germany. Anti-Semitism has frequently been found among groups, nations, and governments that we would not consider to be Christian. However, some of the worst examples of anti-Semitism have been found among those who are Christian, and in most cases those who hold a Replacement-theology viewpoint.

Early Church Fathers

Anti-Semitism in Christianity began with the early church fathers, including Eusebius, Tertullian, Cyril, John Chrysostom, Augustine, Origen, Justin Martyr, and Jerome. All these men were ardent followers of Replacement Theology. These men published theological papers and historical pamphlets, some of which are included in what is known as *Adversus Judaeos*— "Against the Jews."

This toxic stream of venom that came from the mouths of these respected men poisoned the minds of many. They labeled the Jews as "the Christ killers," plague carriers, demons, children of the devil, bloodthirsty pagans looking for the blood of an innocent child during the Easter week, and money-hungry thieves as deceitful as Judas Iscariot.

Replacement Theology was the driving force behind the thinking of these men. These Christian leaders taught that God was finished with the Jewish people. The blessing and favor the Jewish people formerly enjoyed was now given to the Church. The writings of these men reflected this new viewpoint. Tertullian (A.D. 160-220), a prominent church theologian from North Africa, wrote an anti-Semitic discourse entitled *An Answer to the Jews*. He taught that God's statements to Rebekah concerning the twins (Esau and Jacob) in her womb (Gen. 25:23) indicated that Christians would rule the Jews. He said that Jacob, the younger brother represented Christians. Esau, the older brother, represented the Jewish people. He wrote that the Christians would subjugate the Jews and that the Jews would then serve the Christians.[1]

John Chrysostom

John Chrysostom (A.D. 345-407), who was called the "Bishop with the Golden Mouth", was the first Christian leader to call Jews "Christ killers." It was a vicious label, which the Jews have never been able to elude. He was a noted Replacement leader of his day. He often wrote and taught that the church inherited the Old Testament promises to Israel. He wrote concerning the Jews:

> The Jews are the most worthless of all men. They are lecherous, greedy, and rapacious. They are perfidious murderers of Christ. They worshiped the devil; their religion is a sickness. The Jews are odious assassins of Christ, and for killing God there is no expiation possible, no indulgence or pardon. Christians may never cease vengeance, and the Jews must live in servitude forever. God always hated the Jews. It is incumbent upon all Christians (their duty) to hate the Jews.[2]

The Spanish Inquisition (A.D. 1478-1808)

The Spanish Inquisition was perhaps the most cynical plot in the dark history of Catholicism, aimed at expropriating the property of wealthy Jews and converts in Spain for the benefit of the royal court and the Roman Catholic Church. Even dead Jews were dug up and put on "trial" so their estates could be confiscated from their heirs.

When Tomas Torquemada, was appointed by the church as Inquisitor General of Spain in 1483, he printed *Manuals of Inquisition*, which told the citizens of Spain how to spot a Jew or a *maranno* (pig), a term used to identify Jews who converted to Christianity to escape persecution but secretly practiced Judaism. Once caught, these people were to be brought to trial by the Roman Catholic Church.

The trial was actually a torture chamber using the garrotte, rack, whip, needle, and fire to force those on trial to confess their sin of converting to Judaism, or of being "closet" Jews. Inquisition tortures continued well into the nineteenth century. During that time, 300,000 people were burned, and 17,659 were burned in effigy. It is one of the darkest periods in Spanish history.[3]

Martin Luther

Martin Luther (A.D. 1483-1546) may have been the most infamous anti-Semite of all the Replacement Theologians. Dean William Inge (1860-1954), professor of Theology at Cambridge University in England once said, "The worst evil genius of Germany is not Hitler or Bismarck or Fredrick the Great, but Martin Luther."[4]

When Martin Luther introduced the Reformation, he was convinced that the Jewish people would join with him in an assault on the Roman Catholic Church. He was wrong. In the beginning of the Reformation movement, Luther made kind and generous remarks about the Jewish people in his writings. However, when he saw that the Jews did not follow him, his kindness became outrage, and he turned on the Jews with a vengeance that greatly appealed to the German people.

Adolf Hitler read and deeply appreciated Luther's anti-Jewish tracts. His doctrine provided Hitler with many suitable texts for his extermination program. The most vicious, Jew-hating statements Luther ever made were to be found in his tract entitled *Concerning the Jews and Their Lives*. In it he stated:

> Let me give you my honest advice. First, their synagogues or churches should be set on fire. And whatever does not burn up should be covered or spread over with dirt so that no one may ever be able to see a cinder or stone of it. And this ought to be done for the honor of God and of Christianity in order that God may see that we are Christians... Secondly, their homes should be broken down and destroyed. Thirdly, they should be deprived of their prayer books and the Talmud in which such idolatry, lies, cursing, and blasphemy are taught. Fourthly, their Rabbis must be forbidden under the threat of death to teach anymore... Fifthly, passport and traveling privileges should be absolutely forbidden to Jews. Let them stay at home. Sixthly, they ought to be stopped for usury. For this reason, as said before, everything they possess they stole and robbed us through their usury, for they have no other means of support...To sum up, dear princes and notables who have Jews in your domains, if this advice of mine does not suit you, then find a better one so that you and we may all be free from this inseparable Jewish burden...the Jews.[5]

Two days after writing this tract, Martin Luther died! Sadly, however, Replacement Theology's practice of anti-Semitism is still active in the world. The anti-Jewish attitudes of Preterist, Reformed, and Calvinist churches are still with us today. They have softened their methods in our day so that anti-Semitism does not take the form of torture, killing, and persecution.

Anti-Semitism today is the denial that all the promises made to the nation of Israel will be fulfilled. Radio Bible teacher J. Vernon McGee tells of a conversation that he had with an eminent Bible scholar. "Recently, a leading scholar said to me, 'I do not like your Judaistic eschatology.' He continued, 'I do not like this idea that God has yet to deal with the nation of Israel.' I told him that I consider that the very heart of the Bible. Then I asked him what he did with the promises made to the nation of Israel. He said, 'They are for the Church.' Immediately I asked, 'What about the curses that were pronounced on the nation of Israel?' 'Well', he said, 'I don't worry with those.' Never yet have I found anyone who takes the promises away from Israel that ever takes the curses also! They always leave the curses for the Jews."[6]

Why is There So Much Anti-Semitism?

History records that nearly every great nation has persecuted and tried to exterminate the descendants of Abraham — the Jews. Yet the Jews have attended the funeral of nearly every one of these nations. The book of Esther records one of the earliest attempts, led by Haman, to eliminate the Jews. Most recently, Hitler tried to exterminate them in the ovens and death camps of the Gestapo. He thought he would be able to rid the world of the Jews, but he failed. Haman and Hitler are gone, but the Jews are still with us!

Nearly seven hundred years before the birth of Christ, the Jewish prophet Isaiah foretold of the protective and providential hand of God upon the life of the nation of Israel. It is not likely that either Haman or Hitler or any of the contemporary enemies of Israel did or will pay much attention to Isaiah 54:17. Yet, this is God's sovereign oath wherein He has sworn to protect the nation of Israel:

> "'No weapon that is formed against thee shall prosper; and every tongue that shall rise against thee in judgment thou shalt condemn. This is the heritage of the servants of the Lord, and their righteousness is of Me', saith the Lord." (Isa. 54:17).

As one looks back at all the suffering endured by the Jewish people, the question is rightly posed: Why has Israel suffered so much persecution and anti-Semitism? We hesitate to offer a simplistic answer to what is a very complex question. Books have been written, conferences have been sponsored, and numerous lectures have been devoted completely to this very question. Nevertheless, allow me to offer two biblical and undeniable reasons.

Firstly, in the providence and design of God, the people of this race have been designated as the custodians of His divine written Word. The Bible has come to us through the Jewish people. God chose them for this important task. God chose Jewish men in the Old Testament days such as Moses, Samuel, David, and Ezra; and in the New Testament times He chose the apostles Paul, Peter, and John. Satan hates the Jews because they have been the means that God has used to bring the message of the Scriptures to a lost and spiritually needy world. Secondly, it is through the Jewish nation that the Lord Jesus Christ, the Messiah, the Saviour of the world was born. The apostle Paul puts it this way: *"Whose are the fathers, and of whom, as concerning the flesh, Christ came, God blessed forever"* (Rom. 9:5). There is no way of escaping the fact that there is a supernatural hatred of them, because the Lord Jesus Christ was a Jew and because the Scriptures have come to us through the Jewish people. God chose them for this purpose, and because of that they are hated. Satan hates them, and as a result, he has fanned the flames of hatred in the nations of the world against the Jewish people.

Conclusion

The Jewish people have suffered untold persecution down through the ages. Sadly, much of this persecution has come through the hand of Bible-believing Christians. Some of these Christians were heroes of the evangelical church, such as Martin Luther, John Calvin, and others. The church should vigorously reject and repudiate the anti-Semitic writings and actions of that dark period of church history. Unfortunately, history often repeats itself. Today, sadly, many Replacement Christians still harbour God-dishonoring anti-Jewish feelings and attitudes. May they see and come to learn of the special love that God has for the Jewish people!

Endnotes

1. *Anti-Nicene Fathers,* ed. Alexander Roberts and James Donaldson (Peabody, MA: Hendrickson, 1994), 3:151-152

2. John Chrysostom, *Discourses Against Judaizing Christians* (vol. 68 of *Fathers of the Church*), translated by Paul W. Harkins (Washington, D.C.: Catholic University of America Press, 1979), p. 31

3. Dagobert R. Runes, *The War Against the Jews,* (New York: Philosophical Library, ND), p. 171

4. Malcolm Hay, *The Roots of Christian Anti-Semitism,* (New York, NY: Freedom Library Press, 1981), p. 166

5. Martin Luther, *Luther's Works, The Christian in Society, Vol. 4,* (Philadelphia, PA: Fortress Press, 1971), pp. 268-293

6. J. V. McGee, *Esther: Romance of Providence,* (Nelson: Nashville, TN, 1982), p. 71

Replacement Theology, History, and The Modern State of Israel

It was near two o'clock on the afternoon of August 16, 1949, when an airplane flown by an American pilot appeared over the Mediterranean coast of Israel. Immediately, four fighter planes from the Israeli Air Force joined it. Earlier that day, this plane had left Vienna, Austria. It carried the remains of a Jew who had died forty-five years before and whose body had slept quietly all these years, wrapped in the blue and white flag of Zion. The grave in which it had been interred was an ordinary grave like many others in Austria. It was a tall stone surrounded by a wrought iron railing over which ivy had crept through the passing years, making it almost indistinguishable, until one noted something else. Above, below, and on all sides of the stone and the railing, there was handwriting in Hebrew, Russian, and German. These writings were not desecrations. Rather, they were expressions of gratitude felt by the thousands of Jews who had visited the grave since 1904. The writings contained requests, hopes, prayers, proverbs, and blessings. Coming from all parts of the world, Jews had expressed in many different languages their longing for a national home in Israel and their appreciation to the man whose leadership had so inspired them.

Now, in 1949, only one year after the new state of Israel had been formed, the body of the man was being brought to Israel, where it would lie in the sacred soil of Givat Herzl outside Jerusalem. As the plane landed at Lydda airport, it was surrounded by an honor guard of Israeli soldiers, sailors, and air force men, holding aloft unsheathed sabers. The metal coffin, encased in a wooden box and covered with prayer shawl, was lifted reverently from the plane and placed upon a black bier. As it lay in state at the Mediterranean Promenade of Tel Aviv, thousands of Jews quietly passed that coffin in solemn procession. At dawn a vast caravan of cars wound its way up through the hill country of Judea to place the coffin on a little ridge outside Jerusalem. In groups of ten, farmers, businessmen, workers, old settlers, and new immigrants emptied jars containing soil from three hundred Jewish settlements in the Holy Land into that grave, covering the coffin. A rabbi read the *"Kaddish,"* the prayer given during mourning that exalts God and affirms life. Drums sounded. The great crowd, estimated at over one hundred thousand, sang *"Hatikvah,"* the Zionist anthem. On that occasion, Prime Minister David Ben Gurion said, "This is the second most important return of a dead hero to Israel in Jewish history. The first happened over 3,300 years ago when the body of Joseph was returned in a coffin from Egypt."[1]

At last, after forty-five years, Theodore Herzl, the Father of Zionism, could rest in the soil of his beloved land of Israel. However, now Israel was more than just a beloved land; it was a sovereign Jewish nation. For forty years, Herzl's great cry to the community of nations was: "There is a land without a people, and there is a people without a land. Give the land without a people to the people without a land…" For Herzl, the statehood of Israel was a dream that he would never see realized; but for the sons and daughters of Abraham, Isaac, and Jacob, it was the fulfillment of a prophecy from the everlasting God.

History, God, And The Nation Of Israel

The history of God's dealings with Israel is different from the histories of all other nations. When secular scholars examine world history, they consider the movements of nations and the strength of armies to be the core of world history. Church historians, on the other hand, consider the ecclesiastical conferences, church leaders, and the development of denominations and institutions to be the heart of church history.

It is, therefore, remarkable, when we come to Holy Scripture, to discover that God views all of history, whether it is secular or religious history, from the vantage point of Israel. Even the most casual reader of Scripture will discover that the history of Israel occupies almost every book and every chapter of the Bible. God's dealings with Israel are the focal point of all Scripture. Beginning with Abraham in Genesis chapter twelve through Acts chapter eight, the religious, civil, and military history of Israel is unfolded on nearly every page. Then, beginning at Acts chapter nine and running through Revelation chapter three, the focus of the Bible turns from Israel to the New Testament church, both local and worldwide. However, after Revelation chapter five, Israel reclaims the center-stage position and continues as such until the end of the Scriptures. Thus, the vast bulk of the Word of God revolves around Israel, the chosen nation of God.

Israel And Other Nations

In the biblical text, Israel is always in the foreground of history, whether it is through the telling of the triumphs and failures of the patriarchs, kings, and the prophets, or through the movements of the nation in and out of the Promised Land, or through the various reactions of Jewish leaders at the first coming of Christ. The nation of Israel was always on center stage; the Bible mentions other nations only insofar as they had contact with the nation of Israel.

The Scriptures present Egypt in relation to Moses and the Exodus; the Canaanites as the objects of conquest in the Promised Land; Babylon as it figured in the destruction of the Temple and in the captivity; Persia as it brought about the restoration of Jerusalem; and Rome as it had an impact on Israel during the Gospel period. The pharaohs of Egypt, King Cyrus of Persia, Nebuchadnezzar of Babylon, and many other political leaders are all mentioned in regard to their relationship with the people of Israel, whether favorable or unfavorable. Through all these contacts with the Gentile nations, Israel remains the nation around which all biblical history revolves. The God of Abraham, Isaac, and Jacob proclaims, *"Thus saith the Lord God,*

'This is Jerusalem: I have set it in the midst of the nations and countries that are around her'" (Ezek. 5:5).

Israel And God's Promises

The name "Israel" as it is applied to the nation first appears in relationship to the descendants of "Jacob" or "Israel" (Ex. 3:16), and poetically, they are called *"Jeshurun"* (Deut. 32:15). Later, the name Israel was used to refer to the northern kingdom of Israel after the disruption under Solomon's son, Rehoboam (1 Kings 12-14). The descendants of Abraham, through Jacob, are most commonly referred to as the *"children of Israel"* in Scripture. These are the earthly names that are given to Israel to distinguish her from other nations. However, the names that God gives to this people are especially important, for they reveal His bond of love and His future purpose for the nation. He calls this people: God's *"chosen people"* (Ps. 105:6), the *"apple of His eye"* (Deut. 32:10), *"holy people"* (Deut. 7:6), *"peculiar treasure"* (Ps. 135:4), *"My servant"* (Isa. 41:9)—names of love, but also names indicating a divine purpose. What was God's divine purpose for the nation of Israel?

We must turn our attention for a moment to the patriarch Abraham before we can answer this question. The nation of Israel began with the call of Abraham and God's promise to bless him and to make of him a great nation (Gen. 12:1). This promise to Abraham was gracious, sovereign, and unconditional: *"The Lord said unto Abram, 'Get thee out of thy country, and from thy kindred, and from thy father's house, unto a land that I will show thee: and I will make of thee a great nation, and I will bless thee, and I will make thy name great, and thou shalt be a blessing; and I will bless them that bless thee, and curse him that curses thee: and in thee shall all families of the earth be blessed'"* (Gen. 12:1-3).

God sovereignly promises to Abraham personal, national, and universal blessings. Regarding personal blessings the Lord promises: (1) He would give Abraham a great name, and (2) he would be a divine channel of blessing to others. As to national blessings: (1) His seed would grow into a great nation, and (2) he and his seed would inherit the land of Canaan. Concerning universal blessings: (1) God's treatment of others would be based upon their treatment of Abraham and his seed, and (2) *"in thee all the nations of the earth will be blessed." "Pray for the peace of Jerusalem: they shall prosper that love thee"* (Ps. 122:6). God guarantees these blessings to Abraham by using the personal command *"I will"* no less than five times. In these promises, God reveals His unique plan for Abraham and the nation of Israel. Bible commentators and scholars point to at least four different aspects of this plan.

1. **Israel's sinfulness demonstrates the world's need of a Saviour.** God placed Abraham, the best of men, in a most favorable environment on earth. He gave to him and his descendants divine guidance, a fruitful land, and a hedge of protection about them. Despite all of these blessings, Israel repeatedly fell into sin. In their wickedness, they forgot the God who delivered them from Egypt, and they worshiped the idols of the nations around them. They persecuted the prophets whom God sent, rejected His Word, and finally crucified the Messiah of Israel on the cross of Calvary. Israel's sin and need of salvation are examples to us all of the fallen condition of every nation and every individual before God.

2. **Israel was appointed steward and guardian of the Word of God, the written revelation of Himself.** —*"The oracles of God..."* (Rom. 3:1-2). God determined that the world must have an infallible written revelation of Himself, and the Jewish nation was chosen to be the divine "scribe" of this record. The Bible was written by *"holy men of God"* (2 Peter 1:21), predominately Israelites, as the Holy Spirit inspired them. These oracles of God have gone into the world as a testimony and blessing to all nations.

3. **Israel was the nation through which the Saviour would be born.** To Abraham, to Isaac, and to Jacob God said, *"In thee shall all the families of the earth be blessed"* (Gen. 12:3, 26:4, 28:14). Paul, centuries later, wrote

these significant words: *"God...preached...the gospel unto Abraham, saying, ' In thee shall all the nations be blessed'"* (Gal. 3:8). Through the nation of Israel, the Lord Jesus would come into the world, *"of the house and lineage of David."* These and many other texts speak of the first coming of Christ, the birth of Jesus Christ in Bethlehem. This is the gospel, the good news, that "unto you is born this day in the city of David, a Saviour, which is Christ the Lord" (Luke 2:10, 11).

4. **Israel Was His Chosen Messenger to Witness to the World.** From out of God's call of Abraham and His covenant with him, we see God's concern for the entire world. Abraham would be the first to testify of God's glory (Gen. 12:1-3). Later, God would use leaders such as Moses, Joshua, and the prophets as His messengers. God would say unto Israel, *"'You are my witnesses', saith the Lord, and 'My servant whom I have chosen'"* (Isa. 43:10). God has chosen the nation of Israel to be a witness of His salvation and glory. The Shekinah glory, His sovereignty, and His power were all demonstrations of this glory to the world.[2]

God's commitment to the Jewish people began with Abraham and has continued throughout history. Once-formidable nations such as the Moabites, Hittites, Amalakites, and Jebusites, now occupy only the faded pages of history. These ancient nations have risen, made their imprints upon the world, and then left their ruins in the dust of history. Meanwhile, the Jewish nation continues to grow stronger and more powerful, leaving her impressive mark upon the world.

The "Indestructible" Jew

How is it that mightier and more powerful nations have crumbled into the sands of time, but the small and scattered nation of Israel continues strong? She has grown stronger despite battling a host of enemies who were more numerous and more powerful than herself. She has survived each war and every enemy that has tried to rid the world of the Jews. She has survived dictators, persecution, anti-Semitism, *"Kristallnacht,"* the pogroms in Russia, concentration camps in Nazi Germany, and the Islamic terrorism of today. Through it all, the Jewish people have proven to be virtually indestructible. The mystery of the "Indestructible Jew" has baffled observers and historians for centuries. The only satisfactory answer that can be offered is the unique protection of the Almighty God.

However, God's divine protection of the Jews in the world cannot be fully appreciated by simple observation. Providence is the work of God that can only be truly discerned by the eye of faith. This is nowhere more clearly seen than in the history of the Jewish nation in Russia shortly after World War II. In the Old Testament, God had preserved the Jews through the hands of Moses in Egypt, and later through the bravery of Mordecai and Esther. Yet one of the most remarkable acts of providence took place in the Soviet Union in 1953. On March 1, 1953, Josef Stalin unveiled a proposal to liquidate the three million Jews then living in the Soviet Union. Stalin, a paranoid Jew-hater, had executed thousands of Jews in the 1930s, including many loyal Jews who had supported the Communist cause since the beginning of the Bolshevik revolution. Stalin's anger against the Jew was rekindled after World War II when Israel's first ambassador to Moscow, Golda Meir, was invited to a reception held by Soviet Jews. Soon afterwards, Stalin suddenly announced that a "plot" to kill him had been discovered. He explained to the Soviet press that Jewish medical doctors arranged the clever and sinister plot. Soon denunciations against all Jews from leading Communists were broadcast on government-controlled radio and television and circulated in the print media. On March 1, 1953, at noon, Stalin called a meeting of the Politburo in the Kremlin and read to the Soviet leaders his plan for the extermination of the Jews. However, Stalin's evil plan to annihilate the Jews never took place. On March 2, only twenty-four hours after outlining his plans and exactly one week before the devastation would begin, Josef Stalin died of a stroke. He lay in state for a week and was buried on March 9, which was the Jewish holiday Purim.[3]

In the human mind, the calendar dates of the week, month, and year often are forgotten, but the mind of God remembers always. Purim is the Jewish holiday that remembers God's deliverance of Jews from extermination by the hand of Haman in the book of Esther. God is still in control. His sovereign hand is at times imperceptible, yet His divine purposes and ordering are being worked out *"in the kingdoms of men."* The hand of God is still upon the nation and the Jews are kept safe under *"His everlasting wings."* The light of the sun, moon, and stars will be exhausted long before the Lord removes His hand of protection from His people. *"...the sun for light by day, and...the moon and the stars for a light by night...if they depart from before Me...then the seed of Israel will cease to be a nation before Me forever"* (Jer. 31:35).

God's Covenants With Israel

If you were to draw a circle with a radius of 900 miles with Jerusalem as its center, you would encircle almost all of the Middle East. Athens, Istanbul, Antioch, Beirut, Damascus, Baghdad, Alexandria, Cairo, and Mecca would all lie inside this magic circle. Western civilization is largely the result of the history, learning, and traditions of those ten cities. The ancient world was not large. The distance from Jerusalem to Egypt was about 300 miles; from Jerusalem to Assyria or to Babylon was 700 miles; to Persia it was about 1,000 miles; to Greece was 800 miles; and to Rome was about 1,500 miles. However, of all these leading cities, Jerusalem is one of most influential cities of the world today.

How is it that Israel and her historic city, Jerusalem could become so important in the affairs of the world? The key to unlocking this mystery lies in the unconditional promises or covenants God made with the patriarchs Abraham, Isaac, and Jacob. God has given these promises to impart hope to His people (Ps. 119:49). A unique aspect concerning the promises and covenants is that His people never forgot them. Many of the statutes, ordinances, and commands that God gave His people were quickly forgotten, but His promises are different. Promises are not forgotten! A father can give a child many instructions and commands and only one promise. The instructions and commands are quickly forgotten, but the father's promise is remembered, perhaps, for days, weeks, and often months! God knows how important His promises are to His people!

Of the many covenants that God has made with Israel, there are three that are especially important: the Abrahamic Covenant (Gen. 12), the Palestinian Covenant or Land Covenant (Deut. 28-30), and the Davidic Covenant (2 Sam 7:12-14). These covenants establish three important aspects concerning God's future plans for the nation of Israel. (1) The Abrahamic Covenant promises a chosen people that would be blessed by God. (2) The Palestinian Covenant promises to Abraham and his seed the land of Israel (Gen. 12:7; 13:14-17, 17:8); (3) The Davidic Covenant, which was made with King David, promised a "house" (line of kings), a throne, and a kingdom forever (2 Sam. 7:16). All these covenants are unconditional. An unconditional covenant is one which God will fulfill regardless of the faithfulness of the nation of Israel. God's word is His indestructible bond. He has given His solemn oath regarding these covenants. The Lord says, *"My covenant will I not break, nor alter the thing that is gone out of My lips"* (Ps. 89:34-35).

God made an everlasting covenant with Abraham and his seed (Gen. 17:7) to give to them the land of Palestine*. He added to that another everlasting covenant with David about a kingdom and a throne (2 Sam. 23:5). The Lord Jesus is vitally connected with these covenants. The apostle Paul says, "Now I say that Jesus Christ was a minister of the circumcision for the truth of God, to confirm the promises made unto the fathers"(Rom 15:9). In a coming day, the Lord Jesus Christ, as the "Son of David", will sit on His throne and rule over Israel. *"He shall be great, and shall be called the Son of the Highest: and the Lord God shall give unto Him the throne of His father David: And He shall reign over the house of Jacob forever; and of His kingdom there shall be no end"* (Luke 1:32,33).

God does not build up the expectations of His people simply to disappoint them. No, God has not forgotten His people. God's immutable plan for the nation of Israel will come to pass. The promises concerning a people and the land have been fulfilled; however, the terms of the Davidic Covenant still await fulfillment. God tells His people ahead of time what He will do, so that when the promise is fulfilled, we will know that it is God who has done it! Waiting upon the fulfillment is the hardest part of a promise. But the integrity of the Promise-giver enables His people to wait! Following the destruction of Jerusalem in A.D. 70 by the Romans, the nation of Israel had been a people without a land, scattered among the nations of the world, waiting upon God. Israel would have to wait nearly two thousand years before this prophecy was fulfilled.

The Regathering Of Israel

The most prophesied event of end-times prophecy is the re-gathering of the nation of Israel. The Bible predicts that Israel must be back in her homeland for the events of the end times to unfold. The Old Testament prophets revealed that Israel's re-gathering will take place in stages. Israel will first be re-gathered to her homeland in unbelief in preparation for the judgment of the tribulation. Several Old Testament passages highlight the return of Jews in spiritual unbelief as a prelude to the discipline of the seven-year tribulation period. During this time, Israel will be tried in the furnace of God's judgment (Ezek. 22:17-22, Zeph. 2:1-2).

Secondly, there will be a final worldwide re-gathering of Israel in faith at the climax of the tribulation, in preparation for the blessing of the millennial kingdom. We read in Isaiah 11:11-12, *"Then it will happen on that day that the Lord will again recover the second time with His hand the remnant of His people who will remain, from Assyria, Egypt, Pathros, Cush…"* The obvious question then becomes, "When did the first re-gathering occur?" The only reasonable conclusion then is that the first international re-gathering must be the one in preparation for the tribulation. The first re-gathering must be a worldwide, pre-tribulational re-gathering of Israel.

Amillennialist scholars have argued that the "first" re-gathering was the Babylonian return from exile that began in about

536 B.C. However, the Babylonian return was not worldwide as described in Isaiah 11:12. Isaiah describes this worldwide gathering, "...(He) *shall assemble the outcasts of Israel, and gather the dispersed of Judah from the **four corners** of the earth.*"

The Bible predicts that Israel will be re-gathered to her land in the end times and that this re-gathering will occur in stages. The famous *"valley of dry bones"* prophecy, or vision, describes the final and most important aspect of the restoration of the Jewish people. In this passage, Ezekiel sees a vision illustrating the national return, restoration, and regeneration of the *"whole house of Israel"* (Ezek. 37:11). Israel is first restored physically. The physical restoration is pictured by the coming together of bones, sinew, and skin. An army of skeletons comes together bone by bone, each one is covered by tendons, flesh, and skin to become a complete body. But still the nation is made up of spiritually lifeless corpses (37:8).

Then Ezekiel witnesses the final stage of Israel's restoration process. This takes place when the Spirit of God breathes spiritual life into the spiritually dead nation (37:9). Of course, this spiritual regeneration will not take place until the Messiah returns. The process of physical re-gathering to the land has already begun. Preparations for the first worldwide re-gathering have been going on now for about 130 years.

The Beginnings Of The Modern State Of Israel

In the 1880s, the desire for a Jewish homeland began to burn in the hearts of Jews throughout the world. Influential political leaders in Europe and the United States began to support the idea of a Jewish homeland in Palestine. In 1897, the first Zionist Congress held in Basel, Switzerland, captured the world's attention. However, in the years that followed, interest in a Jewish state began to wane. Nonetheless, soon a number of events once again began to shift public opinion. The anti-Semitic violence in Russia, the Dreyfus affair in France, and the wreckage of World War I all served to influence political goodwill.

As the First World War entered its final year, British commanders changed the thrust of their eastern operations from Mesopotamia to Palestine. Christians throughout the world began to wonder if God was directing military affairs in Palestine to provide a homeland for His people. When the fall of the Ottoman Empire seemed imminent, many speculated that Bible prophecy was about to be fulfilled before the eyes of a watching world.

At the end of 1917, fast-moving events heightened world expectations even further. On November 2, Lord Arthur Balfour, the British foreign secretary, wrote to Lord James Rothschild, a leader of the international Zionist movement:

> His Majesty's government views with favor the establishment in Palestine of a national home for the Jewish people, and will use their best efforts to facilitate the achievement of this object...[4]

Barely five weeks after the Balfour Declaration, the Turks surrendered Jerusalem to British forces under General Edmund Allenby. On December 9th, 1917, the first day of the Feast of Hanukkah (the 25th of Chislev) and the anniversary of the freeing of Jerusalem centuries before by Judas Maccabeus, Allenby took the city without firing a shot.

General Allenby was a devout Christian. He abhorred the thought of shedding blood in the very city where the Lord Jesus Christ had once walked, and he had no desire, either, to damage the city's walls. He had brought up his troops, determined to free the city, but wondering how it might be done peaceably. Meanwhile, the rumor of Allenby's approach ran through the Turkish garrison. In the Turkish language, Allenby's name was rendered "Allah bye," which means "the Prophet of God." The Turks, seized with superstitious dread, were convinced that God was against them, and they fled the city, leaving Jerusalem undefended.

Upon approaching the city, General Allenby dismounted his horse and walked bareheaded into the city. When asked afterward why he chose such a means of entry, he remarked modestly, "It seemed to me the obvious and natural thing to do. The only alternative to entering on foot by the Jaffa Gate was to enter on horseback through the enormous hole in the wall made especially to permit the German Kaiser to make what he regarded as a triumphant and spectacular entry into Jerusalem. That was a procedure I naturally shrank from repeating."[5]

Dispensational Christians, more than any others, were attentive to these fast-moving events and sought to explain them as a fulfillment of Bible prophecy. These events, coupled with the bedrock of Bible prophecy, convinced them more than ever that God was sovereignly working to provide a national homeland for the Jews. The record of the past 64 years has taught the world that the Dispensational perspective on these events and biblical prophecy was not only faithful but also historic.

The Zionist Movement, W. E. Blackstone, And Dispensationalism

No American pre-millennialist earned more acclaim among Zionists than W. E. Blackstone, the author of *Jesus is Coming*, one of the most widely read books of its time on biblical prophecy. William Eugene Blackstone (1841-1935) was born in Adams, New York, into a Methodist home and was converted at the age of eleven. After the Civil War, he married and moved to Oak Park, Illinois, where he started a successful business in building and property investments.

In the 1880s, Blackstone became an associate of D. L. Moody and published the book *Jesus Is Coming*. Through his prophetic studies and association with other Dispensationalists, he developed a growing interest in the Jewish people. In 1888, he visited the Holy Land with his daughter. Upon his return, in 1890, Blackstone organized the first conference between Christians and Jews, which was held in Chicago.

The following year, Blackstone's concern for the oppressed Jews in Europe led him to sponsor an amazing "memorial" on behalf of Russian Jews. On March 5, 1891, Blackstone sent his memorial to President Benjamin Harrison and Secretary of State

James Blaine. The memorial began with the question: "What shall be done for the Russian Jews?" After briefly discussing the situation in Europe, Blackstone offered his own solution:

> Why not give Palestine back to them again? According to God's distribution of nations, it is their home—an inalienable possession from which they were expelled by force...

This memorial was signed by 413 prominent Americans, including the following: Melville Fuller, the Chief Justice of the United States Supreme Court; Chauncy Depew, United States Senator from New York; the mayors of Chicago, Boston, and New York, and many other elected officials; leading journalists from the *Chicago Daily News*, the *New York Times*, and the *Washington Post*; businessmen such as Cyrus McCormick, John D. Rockefeller, and J. Pierpont Morgan. Blackstone's memorial was very significant. It must be remembered that it was written five years before Theodor Herzl's book *The Jewish State*, and six years before the first Zionist Congress. Blackstone's interest in the Zionist movement increased even further in the years following. When leading Zionist Theodor Herzl showed a lack of commitment to Palestine as the site for the Jewish state, W. E. Blackstone sent him a marked copy of the Old Testament, highlighting those passages that indicated that the Jews must return to Palestine. Today, Blackstone's marked Old Testament is on public exhibition at the "History of Zionism" display at Herzl's grave in Israel.

Blackstone was a true friend of Israel, and Jewish Zionists sincerely appreciated Blackstone's efforts on their behalf. At a 1918 Zionist Conference in Philadelphia, Blackstone was acclaimed a "Father of Zionism." Later in that same year, Blackstone was invited to speak at a large Zionist conference in Los Angeles. Blackstone's desire for the salvation of the Jewish people was evident when he addressed the assembled crowd:

> I am, and for over thirty years have been, an ardent advocate of Zionism. This is because I believe that

true Zionism is founded on the plan, purpose, and fiat of the everlasting and omnipotent God, as prophetically recorded in His Holy Word, the Bible...There are only three courses open to every Jew...first to become a true Christian, accepting the Lord Jesus Christ as Lord and Saviour, which brings not only forgiveness and regeneration, but ensures escape from the unequaled time of tribulation which is coming upon all the earth...Oh, my Jewish friend, which of these paths shall be yours?...Study the wonderful Word of God and see how plainly God Himself has revealed Israel's pathway unto the perfect day...[6]

Blackstone retained a cherished place in the history of the early Zionist movement. In 1956, upon the seventy-fifth anniversary of Blackstone's memorial as presented to President Harrison, the citizens of the state of Israel dedicated a forest in his honor.

The land of Israel without a Jew was a land without a soul. With the rebirth of the state of Israel, the Promised Land experienced a resurrection. The Jews have returned to their land from the far corners of the world. Where once-barren fields lay uncultivated, today forests, fields, and farms flourish. They have transformed the country, fought off their enemies, and fortified their borders. They have come to stay! These sons and daughters of Jacob have created a small, but strong, and highly-industrialized nation in the most strategic area in the world. From time to time, anti-Semitism rears its ugly head and seeks to harm the *"apple of God's eye."* However, Israel has not seen the worst that man can do unto her. The Bible warns that there is yet a time to come called *"the time of Jacob's trouble"* (Jer. 30:7). All of her struggles and battles may prove to be just a trial performance for the horrors that await her in the future.

Conclusion

On May 14, 1948, at 4:00 P. M., the General Zionist Council at Tel Aviv proclaimed to the world the establishment of the state of Israel. David Ben Gurion became its first prime minister and chemist Chaim Weizman its first president. Israel was now a sovereign nation in the community of nations. This was a significant moment in the history of the Jewish people. Doubtless, the God who turns *"the king's heart...whithersoever He will"* (Prov. 21:1) was sovereignly guiding each of these historic events. Nevertheless, much of God's plan for the nation of Israel is yet to be fulfilled. The prophetic clock is still ticking for Israel. The seven-year tribulation period, the Antichrist, and the millennial reign of Christ are all still future. The day is yet to come when the eyes of the Jews will be opened at last, they will *"look on Him whom they pierced"* (Zechariah 12:10), and they will mourn. Israel will be saved! Then Jesus Christ will be owned at last as Israel's Messiah, Saviour, and Lord. Israel will be a nation *"born in a day"* (Isaiah 66:7-9). The Lord's throne will be set in sight of the dark valley through which He passed on His way to Gethsemane. Then at last, Jewish men, women, and children, joining with Gentiles, will gather around His throne, joyously shouting their praise: *"Alleluia; salvation, and glory, and honor, and power, unto the Lord our God"* (Rev. 19:1).

*The term "Palestine" is neither the most accurate nor the most useful term in referring to the Promised Land. This term is never used in the Bible. The term used in the Bible is the "land of Israel." Historians believe that the Roman emperor Aelius Hadrianus (A.D. 76-138) was the first to coin this term. Many in the news media use this term today to give the mistaken idea that Israel is occupying a land belonging to the Palestinian Arabs.

Endnotes

1. Walter Price, *Next Year in Jerusalem*, (Chicago, IL: Moody Press, 1975), p. 11

2. Dr. Louis T. Talbot, *God's Plan of the Ages*, (Grand Rapids, MI: Eerdmans, 1989), p. 60

3. Harold Willmington, *Willmington's Guide to the Bible*, (Wheaton, IL, Tyndale, 1981), p. 253

4. Melvin Urofsky, *American Zionism from Herzl to Holocaust* (Garden City, NY: Anchor Books,1976), p. 199

5. *Sydney Morning Herald*, 26 January, 1926

6. Timothy Weber, *Living in the Shadow of the Second Coming*, (Grand Rapids, MI: Zondervan, 1983), p. 140-141

Replacement Theology And The Land of Israel

In 1878, William Eugene Blackstone (1840-1935) wrote the popular book, *Jesus is Coming*. Over the next 50 years, *Jesus is Coming* sold millions of copies worldwide and was translated into 48 languages. It became the trusted reference source of end-times prophetic study. In his early years, Blackstone's ministry focused on the rapture of the Church and the restoration of the Jews to the Holy Land. Eventually, however, God would use W. E. Blackstone in the formation of a Jewish state in the land of Abraham, Isaac, and Jacob.

Blackstone and his daughter traveled to the Holy Land in 1888. He returned convinced that a permanent homeland for the Jews was the only solution to their worldwide persecution. On November 24–25, 1890, Blackstone organized a conference on the *Past, Present, and Future of Israel* at the First Methodist Episcopal Church in Chicago, where the speakers included leaders of both Jewish and Christian communities. The Zionist movement was stirring the hope for a homeland in the hearts of Jews worldwide. Soon, Blackstone became the evangelical church's leading Christian Zionist.

Nevertheless, there was discouragement in the Zionist movement. Well-attended Zionist congresses were held, yet with little apparent progress. Zionist leader Theodor Herzl petitioned political leaders of the world, letters were written, and newspaper articles appeared in major news outlets, but again, it seemed that little ground was gained toward a homeland for the Jews. By the latter part of the 1890's, hope for a homeland for the Jews had reached its lowest point. At this difficult time, the British government offered 6,000 square miles of land as an interim Jewish state in Uganda. At the Sixth Zionist Congress held in 1903, Herzl laid out his *Uganda Program*, proposing that Jews settle in the British territory of Uganda. Later, there was an offer of a homeland in Argentina. Blackstone was sure Herzl and the other Zionists would reject these offers out of hand.

When Blackstone discovered that Herzl was seriously considering the establishment of a homeland for the Jews outside of the land of Israel, he highlighted in a Bible hundreds of Old Testament prophecies concerning Israel's land, and sent it to Herzl. Blackstone informed Herzl that his proposal to have the Jewish state in Argentina, Uganda, or any other country was unacceptable—it had to be in the promised land of Israel with Jerusalem as its capital. The Bible was prominently displayed on Herzl's desk for many years. Today, the *Blackstone Bible* containing those marked prophecies is displayed at the Herzl Museum, at Mount Herzl, Jerusalem.

Blackstone not only challenged Theodor Herzl with his biblical arguments for a homeland for the Jews, he appealed to every United States President of his time. He met with or petitioned Presidents Benjamin Harrison, William McKinley, Grover Cleveland, Theodore Roosevelt, and Woodrow Wilson. Blackstone's words so saturated these Presidents, that in 1949, some fourteen years after Blackstone's death, Harry Truman, who represented the U.S. as the first nation to recognize the newborn state of Israel, virtually quoted Blackstone's letter. When Truman was introduced to some Jewish scholars that year as "the man who helped create the State of Israel," Truman responded with, "What do you mean 'helped create'? I am Cyrus, I am Cyrus!" Blackstone's efforts, using the Bible as his foundation, began his crusade for a Jewish homeland five years before the father of modern-day Zionism, Theodor Herzl, published his book *The Jewish State*. W. E. Blackstone demonstrated that the strongest rationale for a Jewish state in the land of Israel is the Bible.

Do the Jewish People Have a Right to the Land of Israel?

There are five basic claims that the Jewish people offer in justifying a Jewish state in the ancient land of Israel. These five suppositions are both historical and biblical. We will explore these five arguments:

1. Their Ancient Residency in the Land

The land of Israel was conquered by Joshua (as commanded by God) in 1405 B.C., some two thousand years before the Arabs came. For nearly fifteen centuries, Jewish people occupied the region. Although many other people-groups conquered parts of the land of Israel, a sizable Jewish community remained there throughout that time as caretakers. This continued into modern times. When the British conquered the area in 1917, Ottoman Turks, not the Arabs, ruled it. The land had been under Turkish control for about four hundred years. Nevertheless, the Jews always counted the land of Israel as their native land and never relinquished their claim throughout their dispersion. They always longed for a restoration to the homeland from which they had been evicted.

2. The Balfour Declaration

An essential part of the Versailles Peace Treaty was the *Balfour Declaration*, which guaranteed the Jews a national homeland in the land of Israel. British Foreign Secretary Arthur James Balfour sent the following declaration to Lord Rothschild, a leader of the British Zionist Federation:

Foreign Office,
November 2nd, 1917.

Dear Lord Rothschild,

I have much pleasure in conveying to you, on behalf of His Majesty's Government, the following declaration of sympathy with Jewish Zionist aspirations, which has been submitted to, and approved by, the Cabinet:

"His Majesty's Government view with favour the establishment in Palestine of a national home for the Jewish people, and will use their best endeavours to facilitate the achievement of this object, it being clearly understood that nothing shall be done which may prejudice the civil and religious rights of existing non-Jewish communities in Palestine, or the rights and political status enjoyed by Jews in any other country."

I should be grateful if you would bring this declaration to the knowledge of the Zionist Federation.

Yours sincerely,
Arthur James Balfour

The declaration gave the League of Nations approval to establish this Jewish haven under the Mandate of Great Britain, which developed the plan partly as a tribute to Chaim Weizmann for his contribution to the war effort. Weizmann was a chemist who developed the "ABE-process," which produces acetone through bacterial fermentation. Acetone was used in the manufacture of cordite explosive propellants, commonly known as "smokeless gunpowder", critical to the Allied war effort. The failure of the British to honor this part (homeland for the Jews) of the Mandate is regarded by many as a significant reason in spawning World War II.

3. The Need of a Haven Because of the Holocaust

The Holocaust became an ominous reminder to the world of its need to provide a homeland for the Jewish people. Without a land of their own, the Jews were at the mercy of every genocidal madman, having no national government to which to appeal for justice. While the Arabs were promised, and received, seven national homes carved out of the fallen Ottoman Empire, the Jews were denied their own land to establish a homeland until 1948. The decision by the UN to give the Jewish people a homeland in the land of Israel was deliberated upon, discussed, and agreed upon by a majority of the world leaders.

4. The Symbol of the Jewish People: Jerusalem

The Jews assert a nonnegotiable claim to the city of Jerusalem. Jerusalem is mentioned in the Bible over 800 times. This ancient city in the center of Israel is home to three great religions of the world—Judaism, Christianity, and Islam. For the Jews, however, it is central to all their historical and spiritual life. For this reason, the new state of Israel quickly moved its government to Jerusalem, declaring Jerusalem to be its capital on January 23, 1950.

The destruction of Jerusalem in A.D. 70, traumatized the nation in two ways. It brought to an end Israel's political life, and it suspended the practice of most of its spiritual life. For a nation whose lifeblood traditionally flowed through its religious ritual system, the loss of Jerusalem and its temple services was disastrous. Without the Temple, offerings and national feast days were halted. No substitute was permitted for these holy days and sacrifices. The cry of the Jewish people throughout all the years of the dispersion had been, "Next year in Jerusalem." The "City of Zion" is essential to the Zionist movement and has always been central to the nation. Jerusalem and the Jewish people are inseparable.

5. The Promises of the Abrahamic Covenant

The Jews have a strong religious claim upon the land of Israel. The land of Israel was promised to Abraham and his seed forever (Gen. 12:7, 13:15). This promise is the bedrock of Israel's claim to the land, both biblically and historically. These promises were not given to Ishmael, but to Isaac and his descendants. God specified even the boundaries of the land: from the River of Egypt to the Euphrates and from the Great Sea (Mediterranean) to the desert beyond Jordan (Gen. 15:18, Josh. 1:4). During the reigns of David and Solomon, the Israelites conquered lands that reached approximately to these boundaries (1 Kings 4:21).

Although the privilege of occupying the land was conditioned on Jewish obedience, the ultimate fulfillment of that promise was irrevocable in both the Abrahamic and Palestinian Covenants (Deut. 28-30). It was guaranteed by the Lord's sovereign oath, not by the Jewish people's behavior. That property was called a *"land that the Lord has given to you and your fathers forever and ever"* (Deut. 4:40, Jer. 25:5, Amos 9:15). This covenant formed the religious basis of the Jews' right to the land in the Old and New Testaments (Luke 1:32-33, Rom. 11).

"My Land," Israel, and the Promises of God

The Bible says that the sovereign God of the universe owns all the land of the world. The prophet Habakkuk expresses this truth, saying, *"The earth is the Lord's and the fullness thereof"* (Ps. 24:1). The psalmist adds, *"He owns the cattle on a thousand hills…"* (Ps. 50:10). There is no mountain, lake, stream, or hill that is not the Lord's. However, there is a spot, a special place on the earth that is called "My land" or "His land." The Bible repeatedly speaks of the land of Israel as "My land" or "His land." This land is not to be divided. It is not to be debated over in the United Nations. This land is not to be given or revoked by the international power brokers and political heads of state. The land is the Lord's alone, and He alone decides how, when, and to whom it shall be given. The land does not belong to the Arab peoples. Biblically speaking, the land of Israel does not even belong to the Jewish people. The Bible declares repeatedly that God has chosen the descendants of Abraham, Isaac, and Jacob to be "stewards," "custodians," or "rightful eternal tenants" of this land.

Stewards of the Land

God tells Moses this great truth in Leviticus, chapter twenty-five. We read, *"The land shall not be sold forever: for the land is Mine; for ye are strangers and sojourners with Me"* (Lev. 25:23). God tells us through Moses that the *"land is Mine"* and that the people of Israel are to have specific responsibilities while they dwell in the land. They are not to sell the land, for they are strangers and sojourners in the land. In addition to the command not to sell the land, they are not to divide the land. Six hundred years later, the prophet Joel implores, *"...I will gather all nations and bring them down into the Valley of Jehoshaphat, then I will enter into judgment with them there on behalf of My people, and My heritage Israel, whom they have scattered among the nations; they have also parted My land"* (Joel 3:2 bold added).

Warnings and Exhortations

After Israel had dwelled in the land for nearly 900 years, they began to view the land of Israel as *their* land. They had forgotten the injunctions of the Lord to be stewards of the land and not owners. In the second chapter of Jeremiah, the prophet charges the people not to forget the original command of the Lord to be stewards of the land. He writes, *"And I brought you into a plentiful country, to eat the fruit thereof and the goodness thereof; but when ye entered, ye defiled My land, and made Mine heritage an abomination"* (Jer. 2:7 bold added). The land was soiled and defiled by the sins of the nation and the neglect of the religious leaders. The Lord warns them that this lawlessness will not stand. His land is to be the dwelling place of a godly and reverent people, and judgment will begin soon in His land. Jeremiah continues and exhorts the people, *"And first I will recompense their iniquity and their sin double; because they have defiled My land, they have filled Mine inheritance with the carcasses of their detestable and abominable things"* (Jer. 16:18, bold added).

"The Glory of All Lands"

Israel welcomes thousands of tourists every year. They come to see Israel's ancient cities and its religious sites, to walk upon the same earth as the King of kings and the Lord of lords. But few would say that Israel is the most beautiful country in the world. Not many would comment that Israel's mountains and valleys are the envy of the world. Yet the Lord views the land of Israel as no man has ever viewed it. We read the Lord's assessment of the land in Ezekiel, chapter 20— it is the "...*glory of all lands.*" The prophet writes, "*In the day that I lifted up mine hand unto them, to bring them forth out of the land of Egypt into a land that I had espied for them, flowing with milk and honey, which is the **glory of all lands**"*(Ezek 20:6, bold added). Trusted Bible expositor Henry A. Ironside writes:

> He described it as "*the glory of all lands.*" One who visits Palestine today may find it difficult to see how such language could apply to it…That which made Palestine the glory of all lands, however, was the fact that it was there that Jehovah manifested Himself, and there at Jerusalem He had set his Name. From Jerusalem the word had gone out into all the world that God the Creator of all things was honored; and so those who desired to learn of Him came from distant places.[1]

Moreover, this land is a land with which the Lord of Heaven maintains a unique relationship. This is a land for which the Lord has a strong love, concern, and devotion. Moses tells us in Deuteronomy eleven, "*But the land, whither ye go to possess it, is a land of hills and valleys, and drinketh water of the rain of heaven: land for which the LORD thy **God careth: for the eyes of the LORD thy God are always upon it,** from the beginning of the year even unto the end of the year*" (Deut. 11:11-12, bold added). We are never told in the Bible that the eyes of the Lord are focused in this way on any other portion of land, or on any other place on the earth; not upon the glories of Solomon's temple, not on the tabernacle, and not even on the church. Undeniably, the land of Israel has a special, unique purpose in the plan of God.

The Divine Plan of God and the Land of Israel

Replacement theologians suggest that God has no future plans for the land called Israel. That land, they argue, is just a mass of rock and earth like many other lands throughout the world. This land, they tell us, has no particular meaning to the Lord. They urge, "Israel has no right to that land—give it to the Arabs—land for peace!" Well, the vital question is not what the world thinks about this land but what God thinks! Many, many years ago, God told us in the Scriptures what He thinks, and He unfolded to us His divine plan for this portion of land in the Middle East. He was specific; He was exact as He made clear His mind concerning the Jewish people and the land of Israel.

Two hundred and thirty years before the call of Abraham, before the nation of Israel ever existed, when God was assigning the borders and land areas for the nations of the world, He apportioned the lands of the world based upon the land He would give to Israel. God gave land to the nations of the world; He gave the Gentiles their land according to, or on the basis of, what he had reserved for the children of Israel. Moses writes, *"When the Most High divided to the nations their inheritance, when He separated the sons of Adam, He set the boundaries of the people according to the number of the children of Israel"* (Deut. 32:8).

God has a divine plan for the land of Israel, and that plan is that the descendants of Abraham, Isaac, and Jacob will dwell in the land from the River of Egypt to the Euphrates and from the Great Sea (Mediterranean) to the desert beyond Jordan (Gen. 15:18, Josh. 1:4). The great Bible commentator Matthew Henry (1662-1714) writes:

> When the earth was divided among the sons of men, in the days after the flood, then God had Israel in His thoughts and in His eye;…designing this good land into which they were in due time to inherit… The Canaanites thought they had a sure title to the land, but God intended that they should only be tenants, till Israel, their landlords, came.[2]

Endnotes

1. 1. Henry A. Ironside, *Ezekiel*, (Neptune, NJ : Loizeaux, 1949), p. 129

2. 2. Matthew Henry, *Commentary on the Whole Bible, vol. 1*, (Peabody, MA: Hendrickson, 1991), p. 673-6

Replacement Theology and the Land Promises of Joshua 21:43-45

So the Lord gave Israel all the land which He had sworn to give to their fathers, and they possessed and lived in it. And the Lord gave them rest on every side, according to all that He had sworn to their fathers, and no one of all their enemies stood before them; the Lord gave all their enemies into their hand. Not one of the good promises, which the Lord had made to the house of Israel, failed; all came to pass.

Joshua 21:43-45

Sir Moses Montefiore, Queen Victoria's financial adviser, was a Jew. He was a towering figure in the social and financial world of England in the mid-1800s. Montefiore is mentioned in Charles Dickens's diaries, in the personal papers of George Elliot, and in James Joyce's novel *Ulysses*. When Montefiore visited the land of Israel over a hundred and forty years ago, he found that the only land a Jew could possess was land for a synagogue or land for a grave. Through the help of the British ambassador, Sir Moses Montefiore purchased a plot of land outside the walls of Jerusalem. It was the first piece of property in Palestine for twelve hundred years to be purchased and owned by a Jew. Today the Jews hold the land of Israel in their hands, despite the relentless complaints from Replacement Christians that the land does not belong to them.[1]

There is only one piece of real estate on planet Earth that God has expressly said belongs to a specific people, and that is Israel. Yet this land is the smallest, most debated, most fought over, most contested land in the history of the world. Since the formation of the modern state of Israel in 1948, careful observers have considered this incredible event as the fulfillment of the promises of God. It has caused many to conclude that God still has future plans for the land of Israel and the Jewish people. Despite these developments, however, there is a group of Christians who think that the current state of Israel has nothing to do with God's biblical promises.

God Is Finished With Israel

More and more advocates of Replacement Theology are using Joshua 21:43-45 as a proof text to nullify God's land promises to the nation of Israel. They portray God as One who, in some way, is looking to get out of fulfilling His promises to the nation of Israel. They characterize the Lord as saying: "I have fulfilled My promises on that one, now I can mark it off My list of responsibilities." They claim that God has fulfilled once and for all His promise to Israel regarding the land because of the statement in Joshua 21.

In the process of making this claim, they either ignore the promises or claim that God's eternal and perpetual promises to Israel regarding her land are no longer in force today. The existence of Jewish people prospering in the land of Israel is a tremendous obstacle to Replacement doctrine. In reality, Israel now appears to have the blessing and protection of God. Replacement leaders want to do away with national Israel, and they think they have found a biblical passage that supports their point of view.

It is not surprising that Preterist-Replacement leader Gary DeMar is one who supports this idea. He says concerning Israel's future:

> The text says nothing about the restoration of Israel to her land as a fulfillment of some covenantal obligation. All the land promises that God made to Israel were fulfilled (Josh. 21:43-45).[2]

DeMar's perspective should not surprise us since, as a preterist, he believes that virtually all prophecy has already been fulfilled. He believes on that basis that the modern state of Israel has no legitimate biblical basis.

Joining DeMar is Replacement theologian Keith Mathison, who emphatically states:

> Joshua 21:43-45 explicitly declares that all the land that God promised Israel was given to them...God fulfilled the promises he made to Abraham.[3]

So have the land promises to Israel been totally fulfilled so that there is no hope for national Israel? The answer is no!

God's Faithfulness and Israel's Failures

A survey of the standard commentaries on the book of Joshua reveals that virtually no one takes such an understanding of this passage in the way outlined by current Replacement theologians. These commentators suggest that it does not make sense to conclude that all of God's land promises have been fulfilled in Joshua 21:43-45. The central purpose of this passage is to emphasize the faithfulness of God. The majority of commentators suggest that Joshua 21:43-45 should be interpreted in light of the promise of God to the nation in Joshua 1:2-11, when they are about to enter the unconquered Promised Land. Joshua is recording the historical facts that God was faithful even though the tribes of Israel were only partially true to their word. The point of this latter section of the book of Joshua is to highlight the unconditional faithfulness of God despite Israel's short- comings. Trusted commentator Matthew Henry (1662-1714) writes:

> Israel's experience of God's faithfulness is here on record... *"there failed not any good thing, no, aught of any good thing which the Lord had spoken unto the house of Israel,"* all in due time came to pass (v. 45)...(here we find) The inviolable truth of God's promise, and the performance of it to the utmost...[4]

Joshua 21:43-45 must be understood within the overall context of the entire book of Joshua, and not simply trotted out as a proof text. The broad context is that Israel was only partially true to their charge, while God was unconditionally faithful to His word. John Walvoord writes:

> The Lord had not failed to keep His promise, even though Israel had failed by faith to conquer all the land. [5]

God's Future Fulfillment of His Land Promises

Why is it then that many Christians teach that the land promises by God to Israel are still binding and irrevocable? The answer to this question is two-fold. Firstly, the promise of the land to Israel was an everlasting promise, given to Abraham and his seed *forever* (Gen. 12:7, 13:15). This promise lies at the heart of Israel's claim to the land. These promises were given to Abraham, Isaac, and their descendants. God specified even the boundaries of the land: from the River of Egypt to the Euphrates and from the Great Sea (Mediterranean) to the desert beyond Jordan (Gen. 15:18, Josh. 1:4). Although the privilege of *occupying* the land was conditioned on obedience, the ultimate fulfillment of that promise was irrevocable in both the Abrahamic and Palestinian covenants (Deut. 28-30). It was guaranteed by the Lord's sovereign oath, not by Jewish behavior. That property was called a *"land that the Lord has given to you and your fathers forever and ever"* (Jer. 25:5, Amos 9:15).

Secondly, the land promises are still binding because of the numerous passages stating that the Jewish people will have future blessing in the land of Israel. A number of Old Testament passages written after the time of Joshua promise a future for Israel.

There are numerous passages that teach that Israel will be re-gathered to live in the land of Israel in a future day. If there were a single disputable verse on this subject that would be one thing; however, there are numerous verses throughout the

Bible that state this fact. The following list is only a survey of some of these verses: Isaiah 60:18, 21; Jeremiah 23:6; 24:5-6; 30:18; 31:31-34; 32:37-40; 33:6-9; Ezekiel 28:25-26; 34:11-12; 36:24-26; 37:1-14, 21-25; 39:28; Hosea 3:4-5; Joel 2:18-29; Micah 2:12; 4:6-7; Zephaniah 3:19-20; Zechariah 8:7-8; 13:8-9. In addition, Deuteronomy 30:3-6 speaks of a yet future restoration in belief. This will take place after the second coming of Christ. Amos 9:14-15 is one of the clearest future-restoration passages in the Bible.

> *"Also I will restore the captivity of My people Israel; and they will rebuild the ruined cities and live in them; they will also plant vineyards and drink their wine; and make gardens and eat their fruit. I will also plant them on their land, and they will not again be rooted out from their land which I have given them", says the Lord your God"* (Amos 9:14-15).

Donald Campbell, former professor of Theology at Dallas Theological Seminary, Dallas, Texas, speaks clearly on the issue in the following:

> Some theologians have insisted that the statement in Joshua 21:43 means that the land promise of the Abrahamic Covenant was fulfilled then. But this cannot be true because later the Bible gives additional predictions about Israel possessing the land after the time of Joshua (e.g. Amos 9:14-15). Joshua 21:43, therefore, refers to the extent of the land as outlined in Numbers 34, and not to the ultimate extent as it will be in the messianic kingdom (Gen. 15:18-21). Also, though Israel possessed the land at this time, it was later dispossessed; whereas the Abrahamic Covenant promised Israel that she would possess the land forever (Gen. 17:8).[6]

Conclusion

Charles H. Spurgeon (1834-1892), the great British preacher and author, was a great friend of the Jewish people. Concerning Israel's future restoration, he wrote:

> I think we do not attach sufficient importance to the restoration of the Jews. We do not think enough of it. But certainly, if there is anything promised in the Bible it is this. I imagine that you cannot read the Bible without seeing clearly that there is to be an actual restoration of the children of Israel...May that happy day soon come! [7]

The Bible is clear that Israel has a national future in which she will dwell in blessing in her land. This will be after she has been converted to the Lord Jesus Christ as her Messiah. However, in the meantime, the current re-gathering of Israel in unbelief is for the purpose of putting God's people in a position of testing, which in time will lead to salvation. *"And all Israel shall be saved"* (Rom. 11:26). If one misses the clear lesson of this biblical teaching, supported by numerous passages, it is only because of a previously held bias. Replacement theologians have shown that, instead of accepting the teaching of Scripture, they are reading into the text their own Replacement viewpoint. Unfortunately, in the process, they give those who seek to persecute Israel a reason to increase their hatred even further.

Endnotes

1. 1. Phillips, John, *Exploring the World of the Jew*, (Chicago, IL: Moody Press, 1981), p. 131

2. Gary DeMar, *Last Days Madness: Obsession of the Modern Church* (Power Springs, GA: American Vision, 1999), p. 322

3. Keith Mathison, *Dispensationalism: Rightly Dividing the People of God?* (Phillipsburg, PA: P & R Publishing, 1995), p. 27

4. Matthew Henry, *Commentary on the Whole Bible, vol. 2*,(Peabody, MA: Hendrickson, 1991), p. 78

5. John Walvoord, *Prophecy Knowledge Handbook: All The Prophecies of Scripture Explained in One Volume*, (Wheaton, IL: Victor Books, 1990), p. 44

6. Donald K. Campbell, *Joshua, Bible Knowledge Commentary: Old Testament*, (Wheaton, IL: Victor Books, 1985), p. 364-365

7. C. H. Spurgeon, *The C. H. Spurgeon Collection, Metropolitan Tabernacle Pulpit, I, No. 28, 1855* (Albany, Oregon: Ages Software,1998), p. 382

Replacement Theology and God's Love for Israel

What one nation in the earth is like Thy people, even like Israel, whom God went to redeem for a people to Himself, and to make Him a name, and to do for you great things?...For Thou hast confirmed to Thyself Thy people Israel to be a people unto thee for ever: and Thou, Lord, art become their God.　　　　2 Samuel 7:23, 24

Horatio G. Spafford (1828-1888) was a wealthy Chicago lawyer and real estate speculator. The Spaffords' were also prominent supporters and close friends of D. L. Moody, the famous evangelist. In 1870, however, things started to go wrong. The Spaffords' only son died of scarlet fever at the age of three. A year later, another tragedy struck. On October 8, 1871, the Great Chicago Fire swept through the city. Horatio had invested heavily in the city's real estate, and the fire destroyed almost everything he owned.

Two years later, in 1873, Spafford decided his family should take a holiday somewhere in Europe. While in France, he received a telegram from his friend D. L. Moody telling him he would be preaching in London. Spafford was delayed because of business, so he sent his wife and their four children ahead. On November 21, 1873, while crossing the Atlantic on the steamship S. S. *Ville du Havre*, an iron sailing vessel struck their ship. Two hundred and twenty-six people lost their lives, including all four of Spafford's daughters. Anna Spafford survived the tragedy. A fellow survivor of the collision, Pastor Weiss, recalled Anna saying, "God gave me four daughters. Now they have been taken from me. Someday I will understand why." Upon her arrival in Wales, Anna sent a telegram to Horatio beginning with the words "Saved alone." Spafford then sailed to England, crossing over the location of his daughters' deaths. According to his daughter Bertha Spafford Vester, Horatio Spafford wrote the popular hymn *It Is Well With My Soul* on this journey.

Horatio Spafford had a great affection for the Jewish people and the land of Israel. His love for the Jewish people led him to move his family to Israel in 1881. In August of that year, the Spaffords set out for Jerusalem in a party of thirteen adults and three children and set up the American Colony. Colony members, later joined by Swedish Christians, engaged in philanthropic work among the people of Jerusalem, regardless of their religious affiliation. "Jerusalem is where my Lord lived, suffered, and conquered," Spafford said, "and I wish to learn how to live, to suffer, and especially to conquer."

Members of the colony, known as "Spaffordites" or "Overcomers," were renown for their deep love and sacrificial service to the Jewish people. From the very beginning, the colony poured great effort into religious education and humanitarian aid. In 1882, the colony extended an especially warm embrace to a large group of impoverished Jews who came to Jerusalem from Yemen. During and immediately after World War I, the American Colony played a critical role in supporting the Jewish people by running soup kitchens, hospitals, orphanages, and other charitable ventures. Horatio Spafford died on October 16, 1888, of malaria, and was buried in Mount Zion Cemetery, Jerusalem. He was sixty years old. Although he was best known in the United States for the hymn *It Is Well With My Soul*, at the American colony just outside the walls of the old city of Jerusalem he was known for his abiding love and sacrifice for the Jewish people and the land.[1]

God's Unique Love for Israel

Down through the centuries, many have displayed a sacrificial and passionate love for the people of Israel. However, no love surpasses the love of God for the descendants of Abraham, Isaac, and Jacob. God's love for Israel is unparalleled in human history. It is a powerful and unchangeable love that stretches from eternity past to eternity future. It is a love that was not deterred by Israel's unfaithfulness and failure. God's love to Israel was not based upon shifting emotions, but upon the steadfast character of God. Love is said to be measured by what we give to those whom we love. The Lord showed this matchless love in the promises that He gave to Israel, in His protection and faithfulness, and finally, in giving His Son, the Messiah and King of Israel. The Lord God unfolded this love for Israel very early in the Bible, when He said:

> *The Lord thy God hath chosen thee to be a special people unto Himself, above all people that are upon the face of the earth. The Lord did not set His love upon you nor choose you because you were more in number than any people; for you were the fewest of all people. But because the Lord loves you…* (Deut. 7:6-8).

The love God showed to Israel was extraordinary. God had chosen to love Israel, not because there was anything special or deserving in her, but because of the richness of His love and wonder of His grace. It was simply and only because God had set His eternal love on Israel. These were the people whom He had chosen to love; these were the people with whom He had made an everlasting covenant. Since His love was not based upon anything worthy in Israel, there would also be nothing unworthy in them that could sever them from His love. His love for them was eternal and unconditional; therefore, it was a love rooted in the immutable character of God Himself.

Throughout the Bible, God has beautifully portrayed His love for the nation of Israel in many ways. He has used the songs of David to touch the hearts of His people with His love. He has used His sovereign deliverance during the days of Esther and Mordecai to remind Israel of His faithful love. He has used His promises recorded by the patriarchs and prophets to stir the hearts of the Jewish nation. But God has also used three Hebrew idioms or phrases in Scripture so that Israel might never doubt the depth of His love. We will look at these three phrases in the rest of this chapter.

"The Apple of My Eye"

The writers of Old Testament Scripture mention the idiom "the apple of My eye" on three different occasions. It is first used by Moses in Deuteronomy: *"He found him in a desert land, and in the wasteland, a howling wilderness; He led him about, He instructed him, He kept him as **the apple of His eye**"* (Deut. 32:10, bold added). Later, in the Psalms, King David writes, *"Keep me as **the apple of Thy eye**, hide me under the shadow of Thy wings"* (Ps. 17:8, bold added). Much later in the Old Testament, the prophet Zechariah tells us, *"For thus saith the LORD of hosts: 'After the glory hath He sent Me unto the nations which spoiled you: for he that toucheth you toucheth **the apple of His eye**' "* (Zech. 2:8, bold added).

The original Hebrew for this idiom *'ishon* (Deut. 32:10, Ps. 17:8) can be literally translated as "little man of the eye." This is a reference to the tiny reflection of yourself that you can see in other people's pupils. Some believe the meaning of *'ishon* can also include *dark* and *obscure*, as a reference to the darkness of the pupil.

This Hebrew idiom is surprisingly close to the Latin version, *pupillam*, which means, "a little orphan girl" and *pupa*, "girl" or "little doll." It was applied to the dark central portion of the eye within the iris because of the tiny image of oneself, like a puppet or marionette, that one can see when looking into another person's eye. In Zechariah 2:8, the Hebrew phrase used is *bavah*. The meaning of bavah is disputed. It may mean "apple"; and if so, the phrase used in Zechariah 2:8 literally refers to the "apple of the eye." Many believe that our English word, "eyeball" may be derived from the Hebrew idiom the "apple of the eye."

This phrase *"he that touches you touches the apple of His eye"* in Zechariah 2:8 refers to that which God will do to those who have pillaged His people. Israel is truly a people over whom the Lord exercises very special care. Those who touch Israel will receive divine judgment and punishment. The individual or nation that turns against Israel will have the blessing of God removed and will face His judgment. This should remind us all of how the Lord views anti-Semitism.

Why does God use this idiom to refer to His love for the nation of Israel? Some believe that it speaks of that which is delicate, easily injured, and the most demanding of protection. This might speak of the nature of the nation of Israel, who needs the protective and sovereign love of the eternal God. Bible scholar Dr. Charles Feinberg insightfully writes:

> As is well known, the eye is one of the most complex and delicate organs in the human body. The pupil is the most tender, the most easily injured, and the most important to the eye. The loss of it is irreplaceable. Through it light comes to the retina of the eye for vision. What a fit symbol for Israel this is! [2]

The apple of the eye is a beautiful, figurative expression of that which must be tenderly cherished as the choicest treasure.

"My Son, Even My Firstborn"

God uses two familial names that speak so poignantly of God's faithful love for the nation of Israel. Firstly, in the family of nations, Israel is God's "firstborn." The Bible uses the term "firstborn" to describe a family's eldest son. Israel was also called God's firstborn son. The Lord instructs Moses to say to Pharaoh: *"Thus saith the Lord: 'Israel is My son, even My firstborn son…let My son go, that he may serve Me…'"* (Ex. 4:22). God did not ever call an individual Israelite a "son of God", but He did say this of the nation, *"Israel is my son, even my firstborn."* The term firstborn implies priority or preeminence, as well as an inheritance. As God's first born, Israel had unique privileges over all other nations. Israel has been chosen to be a channel and instrument of blessing to the other nations of the world. Gentiles were "blessed" only in relation to their kindness to Israel. However, the prophet Isaiah saw a day when Israel would have a "double portion" of inheritance (Isa. 61:7). Concerning this "double portion" John Wilkinson (1824-1894), the founder of the Mildmay Mission to the Jews, London, and the author of the classic work *God's Plan for the Jews*, writes:

According to Deuteronomy 15 in the distribution of property the "first born" was entitled to "a double portion." Responsibility is measured by position and privilege, hence the principle of "double portion" in God's dealing with Israel. Upon Israel's national conversion and fulfillment of her mission, God says to them *"For your shame ye shall have double…in their land they shall possess the double: everlasting joy shall be unto them"*(Isa. 61:7).[3]

Secondly, God tells us that Israel was His *"son."* Before the coming of the Lord Jesus Christ, no individual Jew ever seemed to have thought of God as his or her personal Father. Jesus habitually called God *"My Father,"* which made a great impression on the minds of His disciples. Near the end of His ministry, He charged His disciples to do the same: *"Go to My brothers and tell them, 'I am going to My Father and your Father, to My God and to your God'"* (John 20:17). He instructed them to pray: *"Our Father…"* In the Old Testament, God is only called the Father of Israel as a whole, never of individuals. He is called the *"Father"* of Israel fourteen times (eg. Ps. 103:13, Isa. 64:8, Jer. 3:19).

One of the most tender verses which speak of Israel as a *"son"* is Hosea 11:1, where we read, *"When Israel was a child, then I loved him and called My son out of Egypt…"* In this verse, God begins to speak of His father-love for Israel. He reminds the people that they became His, not by birth, but by adoption. He loved them and called them, and therefore, they should love Him. Moreover, God did not just adopt His people; He also cared for them in the days of their spiritual infancy, as a father cares for a son. He taught them to walk when they could only crawl. He healed them when they were sick. He bent down and fed them when they could not feed themselves. This is the way God describes His love for Israel:

> It was I who taught Ephraim (Israel) to walk, taking them by the arms; but they did not realize it was I who healed them. I led them with cords of human kindness, with ties

of love; I lifted the yoke from their neck and bent down to feed them (Hosea 11:3,4).

Without such tender and loving care, Israel would have died and would have been no more. Beyond doubt, the love of God for Israel is steadfast, sure, and faithful through all the vicissitudes of life.

"Israel, My Glory"

God's love for Israel is again seen in the Jewish nation's most elevated title: *"Israel, My glory."* The Bible refers to Israel as the *"apple of His eye"* and His *"firstborn"* and His *"son,"* but no title better unfolds the value and the high regard in which the Lord holds the nation of Israel than *"Israel, My glory."*

The prophet Isaiah comforts Israel, declaring that the Babylonian nation which once enslaved her would be destroyed. The Babylonian gods Bel and Nebo would be no match for the strong arm of the Almighty God. In Isaiah 46:12-13, God speaks of the Babylonians as *"stout hearted,"* *"rebels,"* and those *"far from righteousness,"* and foretells their defeat by the Persians. God would bring against unrighteous Babylon His righteousness, that is, King Cyrus, the executor of God's righteous will. This would result in salvation for Zion and deliverance from exile for Jerusalem.

> *I bring near My righteousness; it shall not be far off, and My salvation shall not tarry: and I will place salvation in Zion for Israel, My glory* (Isa. 46:13).

God promises to place salvation in Zion and make Jerusalem a place of safety. God will take up the cause for Israel, His glory. Israel shall shine in splendor and beauty because of her Champion, and the protective hand of God will guard her bulwarks and walls. Moreover, in a future millennial day, Israel will shine in her brightest glory. Israel, the chosen of God, the beloved of God, and the recipient of His everlasting salvation, will shine in radiant glory. In that day, Israel will have the glory of God upon her, the glories of God will be displayed through her, and she will enjoy the presence of the glorious God. Therefore, Israel may truly be called *"Israel, My glory."* Dr. Lewis Sperry Chafer (1871-1952), the first president of Dallas Theological Seminary, writes:

> God speaks of the elect nation as 'Israel My Glory'. Israel has been appointed to glorify God. He has chosen that nation above all the nations of the world for His glory. He loves them with an everlasting love. In His plan God has chosen Israel to be a holy and everlasting nation.[4]

Conclusion

The love of God for the people of Israel is abiding, steadfast, and everlasting. His calling of Israel and His covenant to them is a pledge of His faithfulness. He assures, *"My covenant will I not break, nor alter the thing that is gone out of My lips"* (Ps. 89:34). At the heart of His covenant is a guarantee of His love and commitment. Even though Israel may fail and be unfaithful, His love for her remains steadfast. His promise is His bond. Why is it that God remains faithful to His promise? Firstly, it is because God is God! Secondly, it is because He has chosen them to be His people. We read, *"For thou art an holy people unto the Lord thy God, and the Lord hath chosen thee to be a peculiar people unto Himself, above all the nations that are upon the earth"* (Deut. 14:2); and again, *"For the Lord hath chosen Jacob unto Himself, and Israel for His peculiar treasure"* (Ps. 135:4).

Endnotes

1. Bertha Spafford Vester, *Our Jerusalem*, (New York, NY: Doubleday, 1950)
2. Charles Feinberg, *Zechariah*, (Chicago, IL: Moody Press, 1952), p. 281

3. John Wilkenson, *God's Plan for the Jews,* (London, UK: Paternoster, 1946), p. 74

4. Lewis S. Chafer, *Systematic Theology, vol.* 7, (Dallas, TX: Dallas Seminary Press, 1978), p. 206

Short
Papers

Will the Church Go Through the Tribulation Period?

Beyond a doubt, biblical prophecy is one of the most important subjects in the Bible. The sheer weight of biblical references to prophecy attest to this fact. The return of the Lord is mentioned in every book of the New Testament except two. It is mentioned in 211 chapters of the New Testament, and prophecies connected to the return of the Lord are mentioned over 500 times in the Bible. Nevertheless, many believers shy away from the study of prophecy and are confused as to what the Bible teaches on the subject. Satan loves to confuse and distract believers from the most important aspects of biblical truth, which is clearly evidenced in the area of prophecy. There are more competing views of prophecy than almost any other aspect of Bible study. One of the most neglected, and yet important, subjects of end-times prophecy is whether the Church will go through the tribulation. Many believers have never considered this topic, yet our view concerning it will determine our understanding of salvation, the security of the believer, and the finished work of Christ.

The Calvinist View of the Tribulation

Most Calvinist, Amillennial, and Postmillennial authors and Bible teachers argue that the Church will go through the tribulation period. Older writers such as George Eldon Ladd and Robert Gundry have taught this view. Millard Erickson, professor at Truitt Seminary, Texas, espouses this view in his book *Introducing Christian Doctrine*, a standard text in many evangelical Bible colleges. Popular Reformed author Keith Mathison argues for this view in his recent book *Postmillennialism-Eschatology of Hope*. Recently, Calvinist radio personality Harold

Camping has espoused this view in his radio broadcasts. Despite their considerable education, in arguing their view, these men weaken the statements of Scripture concerning the severity of the tribulation and the wrath of God during the tribulation, and teach that tribulation suffering is needed to purify the Church.

Suffering as Christians & Suffering the Tribulation

Although the Church has gone through periods of great persecution and undoubtedly may go through even more intense suffering before Christ's return, we must assert that the Church of Jesus Christ will not go through the tribulation. We base our convictions on the divine Word of God. We must be clear that there is a difference between suffering as Christians and suffering during the tribulation period. All Christians will suffer affliction, trial, and tribulation in this world. It is a fact of life and it is a truth of Scripture. The Lord Jesus Christ said, *"In this world you shall have tribulation, but be of good cheer, for I have overcome the world"* (John 16:33). Later in the New Testament, the apostle Paul wrote to Timothy, *"All those who live godly for Christ Jesus will suffer persecution"* (2 Tim. 3:12). However, this is a very different thing than suggesting that true believers will be subject to seven years of intense, severe, divine judgment during the tribulation period.

The Tribulation and the Wrath of God

The severity of the tribulation is mentioned frequently in both the Old and New Testaments. Matthew 24 tells us that the suffering during the tribulation will be the most intense the world has ever known. *"There will be great tribulation, such as has not occurred since the beginning of the world until now, nor ever shall"* (Matt. 24:21 NASV). There will be dreadful persecution, earthquakes, famine, wars, disease; but the most severe judgment will be the wrath of God that is brought to bear upon the whole earth. The wrath of God is poured out at the beginning and throughout the whole tribulation period. In Revelation chapter 6, at the start of the tribulation, we read,

> *"The kings of the earth, and the great men, and the rich men, and the chief captains, and the mighty men,…hid themselves in the dens and in the rocks of the mountains; And said to the mountains and rocks, 'Fall on us, and hide us from the face of Him that sitteth on the throne, and from the wrath of the Lamb: For the great day of His wrath is come; and who shall be able to stand?"* (Rev. 6:15-17)

The divine wrath of God is mentioned twelve times between chapters 6 and 16 of Revelation. We read that the wrath of God will be poured out without reservation, and *"…the wine of the wrath of God, which is poured out without mixture"* (Rev. 14:10).

The Wrath of God and the Church

The book of Revelation shows us in graphic detail that the tribulation will be a time when the divine wrath of God is felt by the entire world. This aspect alone is a proof that the Christians will not go though the tribulation period. Why might we say this? The Bible teaches that once a person has been saved by faith alone in the Lord Jesus Christ, he will never again suffer judgment for his sins, neither in this age of grace nor in the future tribulation period. The book of Romans comforts us, *"Having now been justified by His blood, we shall be saved from the wrath of God through Him"* (Rom. 5:9). We read a little later in Romans, *"There is therefore now no condemnation to those who are in Christ Jesus"* (8:1). In 1 Thessalonians, the apostle Paul encourages believers, *"to wait for His Son from heaven…, that is Jesus, who delivers us from the wrath to come"* (1:10). This is an extremely important point, for it touches on our eternal salvation and the eternal security of the believer. If Christians are to bear, in some way, judgment and divine punishment for our sins, then the death of Christ on the cross was in some way insufficient and inadequate. The finished work of Christ is not finished after all. Such a notion we must reject completely out of hand. The Lord Jesus Christ bore the full wrath of God for us once for all on the cross. It has been rightly said, *"Christ bore the wrath of God without mercy that we might enjoy the mercy of God without wrath."* Respected leader and former pastor of Park Street Church, in Boston, Harold J. Ockenga (1905-1985), correctly states the case:

> The Church will endure the wrath of men, but will not suffer the wrath of God...Pre-tribulation rapturists identify the tribulation with the wrath of God. If this can be proved, we must believe that the church will be taken out of the world before the tribulation, for there is no condemnation to them which are in Christ Jesus.[1]

The Tribulation and Revelation 3:10

The most important single passage concerning the tribulation and the church is Revelation 3:10. The Lord, in His letter to the church of Philadelphia, promises that He will remove the Church before the tribulation period. He states: *"Because you have kept the Word of My patience, I will keep you from the hour of testing which is about to come upon the whole world, to test those who dwell on the earth."* The phrase *"keep you from"* is very important. It means I will "keep you out of" — the Lord will keep believers in Christ from the tribulation period that will test the whole world. The Lord does not merely say, "I will keep you from or through the **testing** which will try the whole earth." The Lord says specifically *"they will be kept from **the hour"*** that shall try the whole world. This promises that the church will be removed from the event of the tribulation period that shall come upon the whole earth. It is one thing to be kept through the trial, violence, and suffering of war, and it is another thing to be kept out of the time of war itself. This is what the Lord Jesus Christ is telling His Church: "I will keep you from the time of the tribulation period."

The Tribulation and the Bride of Christ

A number of Calvinist leaders insist that it is important for the Church to go through the tribulation period because this time of judgment and testing will purify the bride of Christ. Indeed, the Lord has used testing to chasten and purify His people in the past. Israel was tested for 400 years in Egypt. He also used the forty years of wilderness wandering to test His people. However, is there any indication that the Lord will use the future seven-year tribulation period to purify the Church, the bride of Christ? Ephesians chapter 5 tells us, *"Christ loved the Church and gave Himself for it; that He might sanctify and cleanse it by the washing of water by the Word, that He might present it to Himself a glorious church, not having a spot or wrinkle or any such thing, but that it should be holy and without blemish"* (Ephesians 5:25-27). The purification of the bride of Christ will be done by the Lord in this age before the rapture of the church. When the rapture takes place, the Church will have been sanctified, purified, and made glorious by the ministry of Christ alone. The tribulation will not be needed for this work; her purification will already be complete.

Harry Ironside once remarked, "Will the Lord have His bride endure famine, persecution, beatings, imprisonment, earthquakes, torture and then usher her to heaven for the Marriage Supper of the Lamb, in a bruised, broken and soiled condition — her veil torn and wedding garment soiled?" Never. The bride of Christ will already be in a spotless and blameless condition, ready for her Saviour at His coming!

The Tribulation and Imminency

The writers of the New Testament stress the "any-moment" coming of the Lord Jesus. Theologians call that doctrine "Imminency." The apostle Paul writes, *"Looking for that blessed hope and appearing of our great God and Saviour Jesus Christ"* (Titus 2:13). James says, *"Be patient, strengthen your hearts, for the coming of the Lord is at hand"* (James 5:8). The implication is that the coming of the Lord Jesus Christ would be soon and that this coming would deliver suffering believers from their oppressors. This coming of the Lord would also deliver believers from the wrath to come (1 Thess. 5:9), the Great Tribulation. The Lord Jesus says in Luke 21:36, *"…that you may escape all these things and stand before the Son of Man."* Respected author James

Montgomery Boice (1939-2000) writes:

> According to the Postmillennial view, the church
> of Jesus Christ will go through the great tribula-
> tion. Nevertheless, this view is impossible for the
> simple reason that it makes meaningless the argu-
> ments of the apostle Paul. Paul was arguing for the
> soon return of Christ. This is to be the major source
> of comfort for suffering believers. If Christ was not
> to come until after the great tribulation, then there is
> little comfort in the Lord's return.[2]

Conclusion

The Bible sets forth the seven-year tribulation period as a
time of divine judgment upon Israel, Gentiles, and Christendom.
Yet, the church will be delivered from this time of judgment
because she is the redeemed, sanctified, and purified bride of
Christ. During the interim, the church awaits the shout of the
Saviour, the voice of the archangel, and the trumpet of God.
"Behold, I come quickly" (Rev. 3:11). Perhaps today!

Endnotes

1. Harold J. Ockenga, "Will the Church Go Through the
   Tribulation? Yes," *Christian Life*, February, 1955

2. James Montgomery Boice, *The Last and Future World*, (Grand
   Rapids, MI: Zondervan, 1974), pp. 41-42

Preterism Examined

Reformed theology has long argued for a variety of Amillennial views concerning prophecy. However, since the 1970s, a theologically dangerous viewpoint called *Preterism* has begun to gain influence and popularity in Reformed circles. Preterism, although first propounded by Roman Catholic scholars five hundred years ago, is experiencing a new wave of interest these days, due to the encouragement of popular radio personalities such as R.C. Sproul and Hank Hanegraaff. Sproul openly admits he is a "partial Preterist" espousing his views in his book *The Last Days According to Jesus*. Hank Hanegraaff, host of the radio program "Bible Answer Man" and president of *Christian Research Institute*, has defended some Preterist positions on recent broadcasts. At the heart of the Preterist view is the notion that Jesus returned in A.D. 70 when the Roman army destroyed Jerusalem.

What is Preterism?

The term *Preterist* is the Latin word for "past." Preterists believe that all the major events of Bible prophecy have already occurred. Therefore, they view the major prophetic passages of Scripture, such as the Olivet Discourse and the book of Revelation, as being previously fulfilled. Preterism is the exact opposite of Premillennialism, which views these prophecies as yet to be fulfilled in the future.

Moderate Preterists, such as R.C. Sproul, claim they believe in a future second coming, but still insist on interpreting the Olivet Discourse and the book of Revelation as basically already fulfilled in the past. As a result, they reject such basic concepts as: (1) the rapture of the Church; (2) a literal seven-year tribulation period; (3) a literal Antichrist; (4) the conversion of Israel;

(5) the Battle of Armageddon; (6) a 1000-year millennium; (7) the future binding of Satan.

In contrast to the basic beliefs of pre-tribulational Premillennialism, moderate Preterists believe that God is finished with biblical Israel. They see no prophetic future for national Israel. The fact that the State of Israel exists today is blamed on "ignorant premillennialists" who supported the Balfour Declaration, which eventually led to the formation of the modern nation of Israel in 1948. While most Preterists would insist they are not anti-Semitic, their theology certainly leans in that direction.

The History of Preterism

This view was first developed in the late 1500s by a Jesuit friar named Luis de Alcazar (1554-1613). His purpose was to defend the Catholic Church against the attacks of the Protestant Reformers. He denied the Reformers charge that the book of Revelation was a prophecy about the apostasy of the Roman church. Instead, he argued that Revelation concerned itself with the Church's struggles during its early years. Chapters 4 through 11, he stated, were interpreted as depicting the Church's fight against Judaism, culminating in the fall of Jerusalem in A.D. 70. Chapters 12 through 19 were viewed as the Church's struggle against paganism, ending with the fall of Rome in A.D. 476. Chapters 20 through 22 were interpreted to be a symbolic description of the glories of papal Rome. Using this clever approach, Alcazar was able to limit the range of Revelation›s prophecies to the first 500 years of church history.

However, a more radical form of Preterism gained popularity in the latter part of the twentieth century and is today the most widely-held version of this interpretive approach. This approach sees nearly all the prophecies of Revelation as fulfilled prior to A.D. 70 at the destruction of Jerusalem, except for the resurrection of believers and the second coming of Jesus Christ. It assigns the tribulation to the fall of Israel, the great apostasy to the first-century church, and the last days to the period between Jesus' ascension and the destruction of Jerusalem. The Beast is viewed as a symbol of Nero in particular and of the Roman Empire in general. The false prophet is equated with the leadership of apostate Israel. Needless to say, anti-Semitism is common among Preterists.

Preterist Beliefs

Moderate Preterists link their belief system to a Reformed view of prophecy in which the church becomes the new "Israel" and must bring in the Kingdom on earth in order to prepare the world for the return of Christ. Most Preterists believe the following:

1. Nero was the Antichrist or Beast. There will be no future individual Antichrist.

2. The tribulation period is already past. It occurred when the Roman army besieged Jerusalem in A.D. 66-70.

3. Christ "returned" in the clouds in A.D. 70 to witness the destruction of Jerusalem by the Roman army.

4. God replaced Old Testament Israel with the Church. Therefore, all the biblical promises to Israel belong to the Church.

5. The campaign of Armageddon occurred in A.D. 70. The fall of "Babylon" refers to the destruction of Jerusalem by the Romans.

6. Satan is even now bound in the abyss and cannot hinder the spread of the Gospel. Revelation 20 has already been fulfilled.

7. We are already in the millennium, but it is not literal. Some Preterists equate the entire church age to the millennium. The 1,000 years are not literal but figurative, even though they are mentioned 6 times in Revelation 20.

Preterist Assumptions Examined

The basic assumptions of Preterism rest on passages that refer to Christ coming *"quickly"* (ie., suddenly) (Rev. 1:1), or passages such as *"this generation will not pass"* (Matt. 24:34). They insist that, because of these passages, the Lord's coming must be related to and limited to the first century. By contrast, Premillennialists believe that Christ›s coming is imminent and, therefore, could occur at any moment. Allow us to examine two passages which Preterists frequently marshal in support of their position: Matthew 24:34 and Matthew 16:28.

> *Verily I say unto you, this generation shall not pass, till all these things be fulfilled. Heaven and earth shall pass away, but My words shall not pass away* (Matt. 24:34).

The word *generation* should be interpreted in light of the phrase *"all these things."* Careful Bible teachers have countered the Preterist view by observing that the generation that sees the Olivet birth pangs will be the same generation, which sees the birth. In looking at this verse in this way, the "generation" of which the Lord was speaking was a future, "last days" genera-tion. Jesus was telling his disciples that the generation that sees the beginning of these things, will also see its end. When the signs come, they will proceed quickly; they will not drag on for many generations. It will happen within a generation.

> *Verily, I say unto you, there be some standing here, which shall not taste of death, till they see the Son of Man com-ing in His kingdom* (Matt. 16:28).

The disciples saw the very coming and glory of the Son of Man in His kingdom when He was transfigured (Matt. 17:1-8). This was a preview of Christ in the glory of His future king-dom. However, are we permitted by Scripture to view the trans-figuration of Christ as the coming kingdom in miniature? It seems that Peter understood it in this way, for he writes: *"...the power and coming of our Lord Jesus Christ, but were eyewitnesses of His majesty. For He received from God the Father honor and glory,...*

when we were with Him on the holy mount" (2 Pet. 1:16-18). Bible commentator William MacDonald explains:

> Are we justified in looking upon Christ's transfig-
> uration as a pre-picture or miniature of His com-
> ing kingdom? Yes, we are. This is made abundantly
> clear in 2 Peter 1:16-18. There Peter is describing
> his experience with Christ on the mount. There
> can be no doubt that he is referring to the Mount of
> Transfiguration…the power and coming refer to His
> second advent.[1]

Two Hermeneutical Problems

A. Date of the Book of Revelation

For the prophecies of Revelation to fit into the Roman conquest of Jerusalem, it is necessary for the date of the writing
of Revelation to have been prior to A.D. 70. The language of
Revelation is predictive; therefore, its prophecies look forward
to fulfillment, not backwards. Therefore, most scholars place
the writing of Revelation at about A.D. 95. Bible scholar Mark
Hitchcock explains:

> While Preterism has many weaknesses, the Achilles
> heel of this view is the early date the proponents
> assign to the book of Revelation. The external evi-
> dence for a late date of Revelation (A.D. 95) is
> overwhelming…[2]

B. Nero as the Antichrist?

Hank Hanegraaff writes:

> Nero is rightly identified as the Beast of Revelation—
> the archetypal Antichrist—because of the unique
> and horrible quality of the "great tribulation" he
> ignited. The horror of the great tribulation included
> not only the destruction of Jerusalem and the temple,

but also the persecution of the apostles and prophets who penned the Scriptures and formed the foundation of the Christian Church.[3]

Joining Hank Hanegraaff, most Preterists go to great lengths to show that the Roman Emperor Nero was the antichrist of Revelation 13. However, does Nero fulfill the many details concerning the Beast given throughout Scripture? A careful reading of Scripture shows that Nero falls far short of the biblical standard. Ignoring the rest of Scripture for the moment, the book of Revelation alone reveals the following aspects concerning the Beast:

1. Literally killed and resurrected (Rev. 13:3).
2. Globally rules over every tribe and nation (Rev. 13:7).
3. Has a high-profile accomplice who performs literal miracles (13:13).
4. An image of the Beast is given the breath of life (Rev. 13:15).

Were any of these true of Nero? Not one! Finally, Nero was already dead when John penned the book of Revelation at about A.D. 95. Clearly, Nero is unable to meet the biblical description of the Antichrist or Beast of Revelation.

Practical Implications

Destroys the literal meaning of the Bible. Once you start arguing that the language of prophecy cannot be taken literally, you are not that far removed from failing to take the rest of the Bible literally. Preterists are following the dangerous path of nineteenth century liberalism, which began denying predictive prophecy and soon rejected the literal interpretation of the doctrines of creation, the virgin birth of Christ, His vicarious death, and His resurrection.

Diminishes the hope of the believer. The Bible warns us: "...there shall come scoffers in the last days...saying, 'Where is the promise of his coming'" (2 Pet. 3:3-4). Preterism sets aside the biblical commands to "watch" and "be ready" for the coming of Christ. It limits those commands to the first century believers prior to A.D. 70. With this in mind, how do we celebrate the Lord's Supper which *"shows forth the Lord's death until He comes?"* (1 Cor. 11:26) Is the phrase *"until He comes"* to be limited to A.D. 70? Are we to stop celebrating the Lord's Supper because He already came?

Every Christian should be concerned about the spread of Preterism. Historically, no prophetic view has more insidious implications than Preterism. It was the poison that spread German rationalism and liberalism into many once-vigorous evangelical denominations. May every Christian seek to equip himself to defend the Scriptures from this subtle attack.

Endnotes

1. William MacDonald, *Matthew: Behold Your King,* (Kansas City, KS: Walterick, 1974), p. 197-198

2. Mark Hitchcock, *The End Times Controversy:,* The Stake in the Heart — AD 95 Date of Revelation, (Eugene, OR: Harvest House, 2003), p. 150

3. Hank Hanegraaff, "Who is the Antichrist?" *Christian Research Journal,* Vol. 28, Number 01, 2005, p. 54

Suggested Reading

Tim LaHaye, Tom Ice (ed.), *The End Times Controversy,* Eugene, OR: Harvest House, 2003

The Untold Story: Muslims Converting Worldwide

The mainstream news media has missed what may be one of the more important news stories to come out of the Arab world. Firsthand reports are indicating that Muslims are converting to Christ in large numbers in Arab lands. The news media continues to report that Islam is the world's fastest growing religion. On one hand, this is undoubtedly true. For example, *USA Today* newspaper recently reported that Muslims, for the first time, out-numbered Roman Catholics 19.2% to 17.4% as a percentage of the world population. Muslims now number approximately 5 million in France and nearly 1.6 million in England. Muslim families in many countries, especially Western Europe, have a high birthrate, giving the appearance that Islam is growing. The truth is, however, that Islam as a religion, when measured by conversion increase, is not growing but rather decreasing. More and more Muslims than ever before are becoming disillusioned with Islam. An increasing number of Muslims are beginning to question the validity of the Qur'an and the extremist teaching of Islamic teachers. Many are finding that the mechanistic rituals of praying five times per day, reciting verses that they do not understand, and frequent fasting are not a means to becoming more spiritual, and they are taking a serious look at Christianity.

Every day, thousands of Muslim intellectuals are leaving Islam. They find Islam inconsistent with science, logic, human rights, and ethics. However the exodus from Islam is not reserved to the intellectuals alone. Today many average Muslims are finding that Islam is not the way to God, but the way to ignorance, poverty, and war. Millions of Muslims living in the Middle East, Africa, and Western Europe have already left Islam. This may be just the beginning of a mass exodus from Islam. They are leaving Islam to embrace other religions, especially Christianity. How many Muslims are converting to Christianity? It is impossible to give exact figures. However, a few years ago, a leading Muslim cleric stated that the number of Muslims who have converted to Christianity in recent years might be measured in the millions.

The Number of Muslims Converting to Christianity

Muslims throughout the Arab world are coming to Christ in record numbers. Former Muslim Paul Ciniraj Mohammed of India reports that more than 10,000 Muslims accepted Jesus Christ as their personal Saviour throughout India last year 2007 alone. The Bible Society of India is publishing thousands of New Testaments for Muslims in different Indian languages including Tazi, with their own terminology and vocabulary.

Islam Watch, the largest support organization of ex-Muslims, reports that in Iraq, more than 5,000 Muslim converts to Christianity have been identified since the end of major combat operations. Fourteen new churches have opened in Baghdad, along with dozens of new churches opening in Kurdistan, some of which have 500 to 800 members. Thousands of Muslims have turned to Christ and are worshiping the Lord Jesus in Morocco, Somalia, Indonesia, Thailand, Malaysia, Singapore, Pakistan, Bangladesh, Saudi Arabia, UAE, and Maldives. Moreover, nearly one million Egyptians have come to Christ during the past decade. Recently Ramez Atallah, the General Secretary of the Bible Society of Egypt, reported:

> Egyptians are increasingly hungry for God's Word; the Egyptian Bible Society used to sell about 3,000 copies of the Jesus film a year in the early 1990s. As per the figures taken from the Millennium campaign in 2000, they sold 600,000 copies, plus 750,000 copies of the individual cassette tapes (in Arabic) and about a half million copies of the Arabic New Testament.[1]

In December 2001, the al Jazeera Network, the Arabic language satellite television network serving the Middle East, broadcasted a live interview with a leading Saudi cleric Sheikh Ahmad al Qataani. Maher Abdallah, the host of the program "Islamic Law and Life," interviewed Sheikh al Qataani, president of *The Companions Lighthouse for the Science of Islamic Law* in Libya, on the subject of Muslims converting to Christianity in Africa. During the interview, al Qataani stated that alarming numbers of Muslims are turning to Christ. "…There are now in Africa 1.5 million churches whose congregations account for 46 million people. In every hour, 667 Muslims convert to Christianity. Every day, 16,000 Muslims convert to Christianity. Every year, 6 million Muslims convert to Christianity." Stunned, the interviewer Maher Abdallah interrupted the cleric. "Hold on! Let me clarify. Do we have six million converting from Islam to Christianity?" Al Qataani repeated his assertion. "Every year," the cleric confirmed, adding, "a tragedy has happened."[2] (*Note: These numbers may be inflated to incite violence against Christians*)

Joel C. Rosenberg & Conversions in the Arab World

Journalist and respected Middle East expert Joel C. Rosenberg knows the Middle East mindset and its culture as well as anyone. For over twenty years, he has lived and worked in the Middle East, first as a journalist and later as a communications strategist for former Israeli Prime Minister Benjamin Netanyahu. More recently, he authored the *New York Times'* best-selling book *Epicenter: Why Current Rumblings in the Middle East Will Change Your Future.* His organization and Internet blog "Joshua Fund" are devoted to providing up-to-date information on what God is doing in the Arab world. Recently, he has interviewed numerous Arab, Iranian, and evangelical leaders in the Middle East. Their testimonies describe a dramatic resurgence of Christianity in a region that is extremely hostile to it. Rosenberg writes, "More Muslims converted to faith in Jesus Christ over the past decade than at any other time in human history. A spiritual revolution is underway throughout North

Africa, the Middle East, and Central Asia. As a result, a record number of ex-Muslims are celebrating Christmas this year, despite intense persecution, assassinations, and widespread church bombings."

"Last Christmas, I had the privilege of visiting the largest Christian congregation in the Middle East, which meets in an enormous cave on the outskirts of Cairo. Some 10,000 believers worship there every weekend. *(Note: The majority of these are not Muslims, persecution is still strong in Egypt.)* A prayer conference the church held in May 2005 drew some 20,000 believers." In other places in the Arab world, we find the same pattern of conversion. "There were only 17 Christians from Islam in Afghanistan in 2001. But there are more than 10,000 believers at present. Every week dozens of baptisms are being held there. In 1990, there were only three known Christians in Kazakhstan and no Christians in Uzbekistan, but now there are more than 15,000 in Kazakhstan and 30,000 in Uzbekistan. There were only 500 Christians in Iran in 1979, but more than one million Iranians believe in Jesus Christ today, most of whom meet in underground house churches."[3] Many are wondering why Muslims are converting to Christ in such large numbers.

Why Are Muslims Coming to Salvation in Christ?

Dr. J. Dudley Woodberry, professor of Islamic Studies at Fuller Seminary in California, has been studying missionary outreach into the Muslim world for thirty years. Dr. Woodberry, aware that throughout the world Muslims have been turning to Christ in large numbers, was curious about the reasons for these conversions, especially in countries where the cost of converting is so high. To find the answer, he created a detailed questionnaire. Over a 16-year period, some 750 Muslims from 30 countries responded and the results are surprising.

1. **The Lifestyle of Christians** – The number-one reason Muslim converts listed for their decision to follow Christ was the lifestyle of the Christians living among them. As Professor Woodberry, Russell Shubin, and G. Marks

write in Christianity Today, Muslim converts noted that "there was no gap between the moral profession and the practice of Christians" they knew. An Egyptian convert contrasted the love shown by Christians with "the unloving treatment of Muslim students and faculty he encountered at a university in Medina." Other converts were impressed that "Christians treat women as equals" and enjoy loving marriages. And poor Muslims observed that "the expatriate Christian workers they knew had adopted, contrary to their expectations, a simple lifestyle." They wore locally-made clothes and abstained from pork and alcohol, so as not to offend Muslim neighbors.

2. **The Power of God Manifested** – Muslim converts identified "the power of God in answered prayers and healing." For instance, in North Africa, a Muslim family asked Christian neighbors to pray for a sick daughter; and then the girl recovered. Some converts noted "deliverance from demonic power" as another reason they were attracted to Jesus. Many Muslim converts also reported dreams and visions. Converts also mentioned unhappiness with Islam itself, especially the Qur'an's emphasis on God's punishment and the uncertainty of salvation.

3. **The Love of Christ** – This is the third and most important reason listed for Muslims converting to Christ. Woodberry notes, the biblical teaching that God loved us so much that "He sent His Son as an atoning sacrifice for our sins" is deeply attractive to Muslims. Converts are also attracted to "the love expressed through the life and teachings of Christ." Ironically, Muslims initially heard about Christ through the reading of the Qur'an, but later turned to the Gospels to learn more about salvation in Christ. Woodberry writes:

When Christ's love transforms committed Christians into a loving community, many Muslims (identified) a desire to join such a fellowship. Woodberry's

135

research shows that when the church is being the church, testifying of the love of Christ and His transforming power, then Muslims are drawn to salvation in Christ.[4]

When is the last time you welcomed a Muslim family to the neighborhood, or invited a Muslim co-worker for a cup of coffee? Even though we are in the midst of a worldwide war against Islamic-based terrorism, we must never forget Christ's command to witness to our neighbors, especially our Muslim neighbors.

Conclusion

At the present time, God is moving in a remarkable way among Muslims throughout the world. Moreover, the opportunities to reach the four million Muslims in our own cities and neighborhoods has never been greater. The immigration of Muslims to the United States presents a unique opportunity to reach them for Christ. Southern Baptist Missions researcher Dr. Jim Murk (author of *Islam Rising–The Never-ending Jihad Against Christianity*) estimates that 20,000 Muslims come to Christ each year in America. May the Lord use our gospel efforts to reach Muslims for Christ here and throughout the world.

Endnotes

1. http://www.islam-watch.org/leavingIslam/muslims2Christianity.htm

2. Interview with Sheikh Ahmad al Qataani, on the al Jazeera Network, *Islamic Law and Life* program, Dec. 2001

3. Joel C. Rosenberg, http://joshuafund.blogspot.com/2008/03/big-untold-story-in-middle-east-2008.html - March 23, 2008

4. J. Dudley Woodberry, Russell G. Shubin, and G. Marks, "Why Muslims Follow Jesus," *Christianity Today*, 24 October 2007, pp. 80-85

Suggested Reading

Joel C. Rosenberg, *Epicenter: Why Current Rumblings in the Middle East Will Change Your Future,* (Wheaton, IL: Tyndale House Publishers, 2006)

Paul Bramsen, *One God One Message,* (Orlando, FL: Xulon Press, 2007)

Selected Bibliography

Blackstone, W. E., *Jesus is Coming*, (Old Tappan, NJ: Fleming H. Revell, 1908)

Boice, James Montgomery, *The Last and Future World*, (Grand Rapids, MI: Zondervan, 1974)

Bramsen, Paul, *One God One Message*, (Orlando, FL: Xulon Press, 2007)

Campbell, Donald K., *Joshua, Bible Knowledge Commentary: Old Testament*, (Wheaton, IL: Victor Books, 1985)

Chafer, Lewis Sperry, *Systematic Theology*, vol. 4,7, (Dallas, TX: Dallas Seminary Press, 1978)

D'Aubigne, J. H. Merle, *The Protector: A Vindication*, (New York, NY: Robert Carter, 1947)

DeMar, Gary, *Last Days Madness: Obsession of the Modern Church* (Power Springs, GA: American Vision, 1999)

Diprose, Ronald, E., *Israel and the Church: The Origin and Effects of Replacement Theology*, (Wayneboro, GA: Authentic Media, 2004)

Ellisen, Stanley E., *Who Owns the Land?*, (Portland, OR: Multnomah, 1991)

Fruchtenbaum, Arnold, *Israelology: The Missing Link in Systematic Theology*, (Tustin, CA: Ariel Ministries, 1992)

Gade, Richard, *A Historical Survey of Anti-Semitism*, (Grand Rapids, MI: Baker, 1981)

Hagee, John, *Jerusalem Countdown*, (Frontline Publishing: Lake Mary, FL 2006)

Hay, Malcolm, *The Roots of Christian Anti-Semitism*, (New York, NY: Freedom Library Press, 1981)

Ironside, Henry A., *Ezekiel*, (Neptune, NJ: Loizeaux, 1949)

Ironside, Harry A., *Matthew*, (New York, NY: Loizeaux, 1975)

Josephus, (tran. Paul Maier) *Josephus: The Essential Writings*, (Grand Rapids, MI: Kregel, 1988)

LaHaye, Tim, **Ice**, Thomas (ed.), *The End Times Controversy*, (Eugene, OR: Harvest House, 2003)

Lindsey, Harold, *The Road to Holocaust*, (New York, NY: Bantam Books, 1990)

Luther, Martin, *Luther's Works, The Christian in Society, Vol. 4*, (Philadelphia, PA: Fortress Press, 1971)

MacDonald, William, *Believers Bible Commentary, John* (Nashville, TN: Nelson, 1995)

MacDonald, William, *Matthew: Behold Your King*, (Kansas City, KS: Walterick, 1974)

Mackintosh, C. H., *Miscellaneous Writings, Jehoshaphat*, (New York, NY: Loizeaux,1975)

Marsden, George, *Fundamentalism and American Culture* (New York, NY: Oxford University Press, 1980)

Mathison, Keith, *Dispensationalism: Wrongly Dividing the People of God*, (Phillipsburg, NJ: P & R. Publishing, 1995)

McClain, Alva, *Romans: The Gospel of God's Grace*, (Winona Lake, IN: BHM, 1980)

McGee, J. Vernon, *Esther: Romance of Providence*, (Nelson: Nashville, TN, 1982)

Pentecost, Dwight, *Things to Come*, (Grand Rapids, MI: Zondervan, 1980)

Phillips, John, *Exploring the World of the Jew*, (Chicago, IL: Moody Press, 1981)

Rosenberg, Joel C., *Epicenter: Why Current Rumblings in the Middle East Will Change Your Future*, (Wheaton, IL: Tyndale House Publishers, 2006)

Ryrie, Charles C., *The Basis of the Pre-millennial Faith*, (Neptune, NJ: Loizeaux, 1981)

Sandeen, Ernest R., *Roots of Fundamentalism: British and American Millenarianism*, 1800-1930, (Grand Rapids, MI: Baker

Books, 1978)

Sauer, Erich, *Eternity to Eternity*, (London, GB: Paternoster Press, 1964)

Sauer, Erich, *The Dawn of World Redemption*, (London, GB: Paternoster Press, 1964)

Scofield, C. I., *Rightly Dividing the Word of Truth*, (New York, NY: Loizeaux Brothers, 1892)

Scofield, C. I., *Lectures on Prophecy*, (New York, NY: Our Hope Publications, 1946)

Showers, Renald, *The Coming Apocalypse*, (Bellmawr, NJ: FOI, 2011)

Showers, Renald, *There Really Is A Difference*, (Bellmawr, NJ: FOI, 1990)

Thiessen, Henry C., *Lectures in Systematic Theology*, (Grand Rapids, MI: Eerdmans, 1976)

Vester, Bertha Spafford, *Our Jerusalem*, (New York, NY: Doubleday, 1950)

Vine, W. E., *Expository Dictionary of New Testament Words*, (Old Tappan, NJ: Revell, 1981)

Vlach, Michael J., *Has the Church Replaced Israel*, (B & H Academic: Nashville, TN, 2011)

Walvoord, John, *Prophecy Knowledge Handbook: All The Prophecies of Scripture Explained in One Volume*, (Wheaton, IL: Victor Books, 1990)

Weber, Timothy P., *Living in the Shadow of the Second Coming: American Premillennialism 1875-1982*, (Grand Rapids, MI: Zondervan, 1983)

Wilkinson, John, *God's Plan for the Jews*, (London, UK: Paternoster, 1946)

Wilson, Marvin R., *Our Father Abraham: Jewish Roots of the Christian Faith*, (Grand Rapids, MI: Eerdmans, 1989)

Other books by David Dunlap

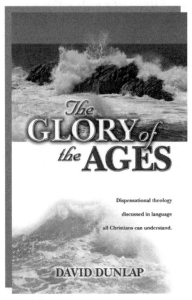

Dispensational theology discussed in language all Christians can understand.

There is a critical need today for Christians to think more clearly about Dispensational theology. the proper understanding of biblical doctrine is not a mere academic exercise but is essential for every Christian. It is spiritual fuel for the soul and a guardrail for the church.

Much in modern-day theology confuses more than it clarifies, and creates more questions than answers. Good theology provides clarity, answers, and commitment to biblical truth. However, the best theology is that which exalts Christ and stirs passion to better understand Scripture, while nurturing a deep love for Christ.

The reader will find that, during the last two hundred years, no theology has touched more lives, stirred more hearts towards evangelism, or awakened more Christians to greater love for Christ than Dispensational theology.

B-17705 • ISBN: 9781897117705 • Pages 256

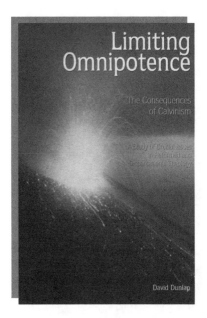

Limiting
Omnipotence

The Consequences
of Calvinism

A Study of Crucial Issues
in Reformed and
Dispensational Theology

David Dunlap

Does theology have consequences? The answer must be a resounding, YES! The theological schools of Calvinism and Dispensationalism both influence our understanding of important doctrines in the Bible. No Christian can afford to neglect the impact these doctrinal positions have had upon the church.

This book contrasts crucial issues in the Calvinist and Dispensational debate today. Its major focus is the consequences of Calvinism. Limiting Omnipotence argues that Calvinism is not limited to the area of election alone, but touches nearly every aspect of Christian life and doctrine.

The aim of this book is not to be overly critical but Bible-based, gracious and fair. Nevertheless, due to differences, biblical and doctrinal criticism will necessarily appear.

Limiting Omnipotence discusses issues in a language that any layman can understand, quoting freely from the Scripture and from the writings of evangelical leaders, both past and present.

B-7000 • ISBN: 9781897117002 • Pages 296

A collection of classic writings and sermons on the Lord's supper.

In the upper room the Lord said to His disciples-*"Do this in remembrance of Me."* If the worship of Christ is the Christian's highest duty, then the Lord Jesus Christ's dying request must be regarded with the utmost importance! Since that day in the upper room, the Lord's Supper has anchored the spiritual life of the New Testament church.

Unfortunately, today New Testament worship and the Lord's Supper are being neglected more than ever before. Strangely absent among true Christians are the spiritual disciplines of reverence, heartfelt praise, and the exaltation of Christ. However, the New Testament charges us, *"worship God in the spirit and rejoice in Jesus Christ"* (Phil. 3:3). The goal of this book is to call Christians back to the heart of worship and the doctrines of the Lord's Supper.

X-8810 • ISBN: 9780967108810 • Pages 64

David Dunlap

Written Aforetime

Selected Articles from Bible & Life
Newsletter from 1993-2009

Today, biblical doctrine that was once widely accepted is now under assault. Many doctrines that were considered orthodox and fundamental are now being set aside by many churches and Christians. The Emerging Church, postmodernism, and theological liberalism have laid waste the once sound evangelical church. In recent years, trusted evangelical magazines, Bible colleges, and outreach ministries have departed from conservative Bible teaching. There is an urgent need for biblical doctrine to be expounded and defended in the church as never before.

Does biblical doctrine matter? The answer must be a resounding, Yes! *Written Aforetime* contains a series of forty-four short chapters which provide counsel, warning, and teaching about biblical doctrines in light of current trends in the evangelical church.

X-1029 • ISBN: 9781607911209 • Pages 362